THE PRODIGAL SON

THE PRODIGAL SON

*An Astonishing Study of the Parable Jesus
Told to Unveil God's Grace for You*

JOHN MACARTHUR

NELSON
BOOKS

An Imprint of Thomas Nelson

Published in Nashville, Tennessee, by Nelson Books, an imprint of Thomas Nelson. Nelson Books and Thomas Nelson are registered trademarks of HarperCollins Christian Publishing, Inc.

Originally published as *A Tale of Two Sons*.

Published in association with the literary agency of Wolgemuth & Associates, Inc.

Edited by Phillip R. Johnson

"Unleashing God's Truth, One Verse at a Time" is a trademark of Grace to You. All rights reserved.

Thomas Nelson titles may be purchased in bulk for educational, business, fund-raising, or sales promotional use. For information, please e-mail SpecialMarkets@ThomasNelson.com.

Unless otherwise noted, Scripture quotations are taken from the NEW KING JAMES VERSION. © 1982 by Thomas Nelson, Inc. Used by permission. All rights reserved.

Scripture quotations marked NASB are taken from the NEW AMERICAN STANDARD BIBLE®, © The Lockman Foundation 1960, 1962, 1963, 1968, 1971, 1972, 1973, 1975, 1977, 1995. Used by permission.

Scripture quotations marked KJV are taken from the KING JAMES VERSION. Public domain.

ISBN 978-1-4002-0268-3 (trade paper)

Library of Congress Cataloging-in-Publication Data

MacArthur, John, 1939–
    A tale of two sons : the inside story of a father, his sons, and a shocking murder / John MacArthur.
        p. cm.
    Includes bibliographical references.
    ISBN 978-0-7852-6268-8 (hardcover)
    ISBN 978-1-4002-8006-3 (IE)
    1. Prodigal son (Parable) 2. Bible. N.T. Luke XV, 11-32—Criticism, interpretation, etc. I. Title.
BT378.P8M23 2008
226.8'06—dc22   2007051511

Printed in the United States of America

10 11 12 13 14 RRD 6 5 4 3 2

To my sons, Matthew and Mark, who have never subjected their dad to any of the griefs and heartaches of the Prodigal's father. Their faithful love for Christ and their abiding affection for their father are vivid, living, daily reminders to me of how blessed my life has been.

❦ CONTENTS ❧

PART 4
THE ELDER BROTHER

PART 5
THE EPILOGUE

❧ ACKNOWLEDGMENTS ❧

NONE OF MY BOOKS WOULD BE POSSIBLE WITHOUT A tremendous amount of assistance from various editors, coworkers, and friends who contribute long hours of their own labor to see a book like this come to fruition. I'm grateful for the team at Thomas Nelson, whose passion and clear vision for the potential of this work have helped shape the project and keep it moving along from the very start. My most heartfelt thanks and deepest appreciation also go to Robert Wolgemuth, whose creative insight and vast understanding of the publishing industry are as helpful to me as his friendship is precious. Likewise I am thankful for Phil Johnson, who managed the process of translating this material from the original sermon transcripts into a workable book manuscript. Phil has now worked alongside me in that capacity to edit more than fifty books over the past quarter-century.

I want to acknowledge my indebtedness to Kenneth E. Bailey, whose books *Finding the Lost Cultural Keys to Luke 15* (St. Louis: Concordia, 1992); *The Cross and the Prodigal* (St. Louis: Concordia, 1973); and *Poet & Peasant* (Grand Rapids: Eerdmans, 1976) were particularly helpful in my preparation for the original sermons on which the material in this book is based.

As always, I'm profoundly thankful *for* and grateful *to* the people of Grace Community Church and the many supportive loved ones the Lord has graciously surrounded me with—especially my beloved wife, Patricia; our children; their spouses; and our cherished grandchildren. Without their long-suffering and faithful encouragement (despite the many inconveniences they suffer during those long hours when I am immersed in study and writing), I could not endure the rigors of writing in addition to my other ministry duties.

The Lord has been unspeakably gracious to me.

—John MacArthur

❦ INTRODUCTION ❧
An Unforgettable Tale

MOST PEOPLE TODAY ARE SOMEWHAT FAMILIAR WITH the parable of the prodigal son, found in Luke 15:11–32. Even those who know next to nothing else about the Bible know something about this tale. Its themes and its language are deeply ingrained in our spiritual and literary traditions.

Shakespeare, for instance, borrowed plot points and motifs from the parable of the prodigal son and adapted them in *The Merchant of Venice* and *Henry IV*. The Bard also alluded to this parable repeatedly in his other dramas. Arthur Sullivan used the exact words of the biblical text as the basis of an oratorio titled *The Prodigal Son*, Sergei Prokofiev cast the plot in ballet form, and Benjamin Britten turned the story into an opera. At the opposite end of the musical spectrum, country singer Hank Williams recorded a song called "The Prodigal Son," comparing the prodigal's homecoming to the joys of heaven. The world's great art museums are well stocked with works featuring scenes from the prodigal son's experience, including famous drawings and paintings by Rembrandt, Rubens, Dürer, and many others.

Contemporary language is likewise full of words and imagery borrowed from the familiar parable. It is fairly common to hear a wayward child referred to as "a prodigal son" (or daughter). People also sometimes speak of "killing the fatted calf" (a metaphor suitable for any extravagant celebration); "feeding on husks" (referring to the consumption of trivial, shallow, or worldly things that can't really give nourishment); or "riotous living" (meaning a dissolute or extravagant lifestyle). Perhaps you have heard or read those allusions without recognizing their source. They are borrowed directly from the King James version of this best known of Jesus' parables.

A Story to Remember

The parable of the prodigal son is one of several memorable parables recorded only in Luke's Gospel. It stands out as the choicest of these parables for many reasons.

Of all Jesus' parables, this one is the most richly detailed, powerfully dramatic, and intensely personal. It's full of emotion—ranging from sadness, to triumph, to a sense of shock, and finally to an unsettling wish for more closure. The characters are familiar, so it's easy for people to identify with the prodigal, to feel the father's grief, and yet still (in some degree) sympathize with the elder brother—all at the same time. The story is memorable on many levels, not the least of which is the gritty imagery Jesus invokes. The description of the prodigal as so desperately hungry he was willing to eat husks scavenged from swine food, for instance, graphically depicts his youthful dissolution in a way that was unspeakably revolting to His Jewish audience.

> Of all Jesus' parables, this one is the most richly detailed, powerfully dramatic, and intensely personal.

Another thing that makes this tale unforgettable is the poignancy demonstrated in the father's response when his lost son returns. The father's rejoicing was rich with tender compassion. The younger son, who had left heedless and insolent, shattering his father's hopes for him, came back an utterly broken man. Heartbroken and no doubt deeply wounded by his younger son's foolish rebellion, the father nevertheless expressed pure joy, unmingled with any hint of bitterness, when his wayward son came dragging home. Who would not be moved by that kind of love?

Yet the elder son in the parable was *not* the least bit moved by his father's love. His steely-hearted resentment over the father's mercy to his brother contrasts starkly with the dominant theme of Luke 15, which is the great joy in heaven over the return of the lost. The central message of the parable, then, is an urgent and sobering entreaty to hard-hearted listeners whose attitudes exactly mirrored the elder brother's. The parable of the prodigal son is not a warm and fuzzy feel-good message, but it is a powerful wake-up call with a very earnest warning.

> The parable of the prodigal son is not a warm and fuzzy feel-good message, but it is a powerful wake-up call with a very earnest warning.

That point must not be lost in our understanding and appreciation of this beloved parable. Unfortunately, the lesson of the elder brother is often overlooked in many of the popular retellings. And yet it is, after all, the main reason Jesus told the parable.

INTERPRETING JESUS' PARABLES

A good rule for interpreting any parable is to keep focused on the central lesson. It's not a good idea to try to milk meaning out of every incidental detail in a parable. Medieval theologians were notorious for that. They might expound for hours on the minute particulars of every parable, trying to find very detailed, symbolic, spiritual meanings in every feature of the story—sometimes while virtually ignoring the real point of the parable. That's a dangerous way to handle any scripture. But it is an especially easy mistake to fall into when it comes to interpreting the various figures of speech in the Bible. Parables are plainly and purposely figurative, but they are not *allegories*, in which every detail carries some kind of symbolism. A parable is a simple metaphor or simile conveyed in story form. It is first and foremost a *comparison*. "The kingdom of heaven is *like* [this thing or that] . . ." (see, for example, Matthew 13:31, 33, 44–45, 47, 52; 20:1; 22:2).

> A parable is a simple metaphor or simile conveyed in story form. It is first and foremost a *comparison*.

The word *parable* is transliterated from a Greek word that literally speaks of something placed alongside something else for the purpose of pointing out the likeness or making an important association between the two things. It's a basic literary form with a very specific purpose: to make a focused analogy through an interesting word picture or story. Interpreters of the parables will always do well to bear that in mind and avoid looking for complex symbolism, multiple layers of meaning, or abstruse lessons in the peripheral details of the parables.

The parable of the prodigal son, because of the richness of its detail, has perhaps been subjected to more fanciful interpretations than any other parable. I've seen commentators spend page after page expounding on the supposed spiritual and allegorical significance of such incidental features as the swine's leftovers (symbolic of evil thoughts, according to one writer), the ring the father placed on the son's finger (a graphic yet esoteric picture of the mystery of the Trinity, if we accept the ruminations of another commentator), or the shoes placed on the prodigal's feet (these represent the gospel, yet another exegete insists, drawing on Ephesians 6:15 for proof).

As a method of biblical interpretation, that kind of allegorization has been employed to create more confusion about the plain meaning of Scripture than any other hermeneutical device. If you can freely say *this* really means *that* and one thing is a symbol for something else based on no contextual clues but wholly invented in the interpreter's imagination—and especially if you are willing to do that with layer after layer of detail in the biblical narrative—then you can ultimately make the Bible mean anything you choose.

The invention of fanciful and allegorical meanings is never a valid approach to interpreting *any* portion of Scripture. And the obviously figurative elements in a parable don't change the rules of interpretation or give us license to invent meaning. In fact, when handling the symbolism of a parable, it is particularly important to keep the central point and the immediate context in clear focus and resist flights of imaginative fancy.

THE CENTRAL LESSON OF THE PRODIGAL SON

That said, the parable of the prodigal son, because of the peculiar fullness of its descriptive details, invites closer scrutiny and analysis than a single-sentence parable. This story gives us an extraordinarily lifelike portrait, rich with fine-brush textures, and these details are extremely valuable in helping us make sense of the cultural context. The details are provided not to add multiple layers of spiritual meaning to the parable's central lesson but to highlight the lesson itself by making it come alive. The interpretation of the parable is therefore fairly simple, as long as we see the cultural imagery for what it is and do our best to read the story through the lens of first-century agrarian village life.

That is precisely what the picturesque features in this parable help us do.

This parable spreads itself across twenty-two verses in this pivotal chapter in Luke's Gospel. With so much lavish coloring, dramatic pathos, and fine detail carefully woven into this word picture, it seems clear that the vividness of the parable is deliberately designed to highlight the parable's central meaning. We're expected to notice and make good sense of the personalities and plot turns in this amazing story.

Indeed, the context of Luke 15, with its theme of heavenly joy over earthly repentance, makes perfect sense of all the major features of the parable. The prodigal represents a typical sinner who comes to repentance. The father's patience, love, generosity, and delight over the son's return are clear and perfect emblems of divine grace. The prodigal's heart change is a picture of what true repentance should look like. And the elder brother's cold indifference—the real focal point of the story, as it turns out—is a vivid representation of the same evil hypocrisy Jesus was confronting in the hearts of the hostile scribes and Pharisees to whom He told the parable in the first place (Luke 15:2). They bitterly resented the sinners and tax collectors who drew near to Jesus (v. 1), and they tried to paper over their fleshly indignation with religious pretense. But their attitudes betrayed their unbelief and self-centeredness. Jesus' parable ripped the mask off their hypocrisy.

This, then, is the central and culminating lesson of the parable: Jesus is pointing out the stark contrast between God's own delight in the redemption of sinners and the Pharisees' inflexible hostility toward those same sinners. Keeping that lesson fixed firmly in view, we can legitimately draw from the larger story (as Jesus unfolds it) several profound lessons about grace, forgiveness, repentance, and the heart of God toward sinners. Those elements are all so conspicuous in the parable that almost everyone should be able to recognize them.

A REMINDER OF GOD'S GRACE

I've always loved this parable and have long desired to write a book about it. But in the wisdom of God's providence, I did not have the opportunity to preach my way exhaustively through the Gospel of Luke until I had already preached sermons and written commentaries on virtually all the rest of the New Testament.

Looking back on my years of ministry until now, I am glad for the Lord's timing. Coming to this familiar, favorite parable after meticulously combing through the rest of the New Testament, I appreciate more than ever its carefully textured message. I approach the parable with a profound appreciation for the glory of the gospel's simplicity, the unfathomable riches of God's grace, the disturbing depth of human depravity, the beauty of divine and gracious salvation, and the sheer wonder of heaven's joy. All those elements are major New Testament themes. No wonder: they are also the core ideas of the gospel. And they are all here in living color. That is, I suppose, the main reason Jesus invested so much time and careful detail in the telling of this parable.

All of those would be ample reasons for working our way through a serious book-length study of these twenty-two verses that dominate Luke 15. But there's this as well: the parable of the prodigal son is a mirror for every human heart and conscience.

SEEING OURSELVES IN THE PARABLE

There's a good reason this short story pulls at the heartstrings of so many hearers. We recognize ourselves in it. The parable reminds us of the most painful aspects of the human condition, and those who take an honest look will recognize themselves.

For believers, the Prodigal Son is a humbling reminder of who we are and how much we owe to divine grace.

For those who are conscious of their own guilt but are still unrepentant, the Prodigal's life is a searing reminder of the wages of sin, the duty of the sinner to repent, and the goodness of God that accompanies authentic repentance.

For sinners coming to repentance, the father's eager welcome and costly generosity are reminders that God's grace and goodness are inexhaustible.

For heedless unbelievers (especially those like the scribes and Pharisees, who use external righteousness as a mask for unrighteous hearts), the elder brother is a reminder that neither a show of religion nor the pretense of respectability is a valid substitute for redemption.

> There's a good reason this short story pulls at the heartstrings of so many hearers. We recognize ourselves in it.

For all of us, the elder brother's attitude is a powerful warning, showing how easily and how subtly unbelief can masquerade as faithfulness.

Regardless of which of those categories you fall into, my prayer for you as you read this book is that the Lord will use it to minister grace to your heart. If you are a believer, may you bask in the Father's joy over the salvation of the lost. May you gain a new appreciation for the beauty and the glory of God's plan of redemption. And may you also be encouraged and better equipped to participate in the work of spreading the gospel.

May readers who, like the Prodigal, have come to the end of themselves be motivated to abandon the husks of this world. And above all, may this message sound a reveille in the hearts of any who need to be awakened to the awful reality of their own sin and the glorious promise of redemption in Christ.

PART 1

The Parable

~

A certain man had two sons. And the younger of them said to his father, "Father, give me the portion of goods that falls to me." So he divided to them his livelihood.

And not many days after, the younger son gathered all together, journeyed to a far country, and there wasted his possessions with prodigal living. But when he had spent all, there arose a severe famine in that land, and he began to be in want. Then he went and joined himself to a citizen of that country, and he sent him into his fields to feed swine. And he would gladly have filled his stomach with the pods that the swine ate, and no one gave him anything.

But when he came to himself, he said, "How many of my father's hired servants have bread enough and to spare, and I perish with hunger! I will arise and go to my father, and will say to him, 'Father, I have sinned against heaven and before you, and I am no longer worthy to be called your son. Make me like one of your hired servants.'"

And he arose and came to his father. But when he was still a great way off, his father saw him and had compassion, and ran and fell on his neck and kissed him.

And the son said to him, "Father, I have sinned against heaven and in your sight, and am no longer worthy to be called your son."

But the father said to his servants, "Bring out the best robe and put it on him, and put a ring on his hand and sandals on his feet. And bring the fatted calf here and kill it, and let us eat and be merry; for this my son was dead and is alive again; he was lost and is found." And they began to be merry.

Now his older son was in the field. And as he came and drew near to the house, he heard music and dancing. So he called one of the servants and asked what these things meant.

And he said to him, "Your brother has come, and because he has received him safe and sound, your father has killed the fatted calf."

But he was angry and would not go in. Therefore his father came out and pleaded with him. So he answered and said to his father, "Lo, these many years I have been serving you; I never transgressed your commandment at any time; and yet you never gave me a young goat, that I might make merry with my friends. But as soon as this son of yours came, who has devoured your livelihood with harlots, you killed the fatted calf for him."

And he said to him, "Son, you are always with me, and all that I have is yours. It was right that we should make merry and be glad, for your brother was dead and is alive again, and was lost and is found."

—Luke 15:11–32

❦ ONE ❧

Greatest Short Story. Ever.

A certain man had two sons . . .

—Luke 15:11

CHARLES DICKENS (WHO COULD SPIN A FAIR YARN HIM-self) famously called the parable of the prodigal son the greatest short story ever written. He joins a large chorus of literary geniuses, ranging from William Shakespeare to Garrison Keillor, who expressed admiration for the parable as literature.

Make no mistake: the prodigal son parable is indeed a model of great literature on multiple levels. It is without dispute one of the finest examples of storytelling ever—with its penetrating appeal to hearers' emotions and imaginations; its succinct, tightly crafted form; and its powerful and person-ally engaging message. It is a gem of concise character and plot develop-ment. It manages to leave a lasting impression on most hearers without resorting to maudlin or sensational gimmickry. The parable is focused, clear, colorful, and full of familiar

> The prodigal son parable is indeed a model of great literature on multiple levels.

real-life imagery. The message is so simple that even a child can fol-low the story line, yet it is profound enough to have been the sub-ject of several classic book-length studies.

Of course, the purpose of the parable in the first place was not merely literary, and in its original form it was not even a written work at all. It was delivered orally to an audience that included (on the one hand) a mix of corrupt tax collectors and some of society's most down-and-out sinners who were eager to hear Jesus' good news—along with (on the other hand) a hostile group of hyperreligious Pharisees and scribes who were angry with Jesus and grumbled that He "receives sinners and eats with them" (Luke 15:1–2). Jesus' answer to their complaint was bound up in the lesson of the prodigal son. The parable therefore had a polemic purpose, delivering a sophisticated and well-aimed rebuke at the religious elite of Jesus' day.

> If we understand the parable correctly, its *spiritual lessons* leave a far more indelible impression on our hearts and minds than any literary analysis of the parable could accomplish.

So despite all that might be said to extol the literary form of this parable, Jesus' intention in telling the story was not to impress His hearers with dramatic artistry. Rather, if we understand the parable correctly, its *spiritual lessons* leave a far more indelible impression on our hearts and minds than any literary analysis of the parable could accomplish. It is therefore of paramount importance to grasp the story's meaning accurately—in its original context and with all the nuances and implications Jesus' original audience would have heard.

CULTURE AND CONTEXT

Let's remind ourselves at the outset that the Bible is an ancient Middle Eastern book. Biblical narratives were set in old-style Semitic civilizations very distant from today's Western world. The complex customs of those cultures are not always obvious to the twenty-first-century reader living in an industrialized society rooted in European customs. In fact, despite the ready availability of mass communication today, the typical Christian in the West has little firsthand experience with life in the Middle East, either ancient or modern.

That ignorance often has a detrimental effect on the way Scripture is understood and applied in popular evangelicalism. It is all too easy to rip biblical stories out of their original contexts, force them into a postmodern frame of reference, and miss their full import. Besides that, one of the sad realities of our culture is that we tend to be in a hurry, even when we read the Bible. We want to find practical applications for ourselves hastily, without doing the careful work necessary to interpret Scripture correctly.

Even worse, in a relentless effort to make Scripture seem as contemporary as possible, Bible teachers sometimes deliberately twist, downplay, or ignore the historical context of Scripture. That kind of superficial treatment has been all too common in the popular handling of the prodigal son parable. It leads inevitably to misinterpretation and misapplication, utterly missing the central message Jesus intended to convey. And that is no small matter.

Surely *this* parable deserves more serious consideration. It is the longest of Jesus' parables precisely because it contains nuances, subtleties, cultural attitudes, and other features that illuminate its meaning more fully. Careful study here yields rich rewards.

Bear in mind, too, that the meaning of Scripture is not fluid. The truth of the Bible doesn't change with time or mean different things in different cultures. Whatever the text meant when it was originally written, it still means today. Whatever Jesus intended to communicate to His listeners when He told this parable, that meaning still constitutes its only true message. (See the appendix for a more thorough discussion of this point.)

> Whatever Jesus intended to communicate to His listeners when He told this parable, that meaning still constitutes its only true message.

So if we expect to draw out of this parable what God wants us to learn and what He intended to reveal for our edification, we need to try to hear it the way Jesus' original audience heard it.

When Jesus spoke, "the common people heard Him gladly" (Mark 12:37)—in large part because He spoke their language. He resonated with their culture. He lived and ministered among Middle Eastern peasant people, and the Gospel record reflects that context. Even the most educated people of Jesus' time would be familiar with the conventions of agrarian village life, because the mores and customs that governed society had been imbedded for generations in the common people's sensibilities. (Some of the features of that culture and its social structures still exist even today in Middle Eastern village life.) Such customs governed their way of life, determined their manner of thinking, and therefore shaped their emotional response to a story like the prodigal son.

In Jesus' telling of this parable, for example, He did not explicitly state that the father was a wealthy man, but (as we'll see in our study of the text) He included enough incidental details in the narrative to make that fact inescapably clear. The fact that this man had hired servants and a fatted calf at his disposal would not have escaped the mind of any listener in that culture. Jesus' hearers all would have the clear mental picture of an important nobleman, even without any exposition of that particular point. Moreover, their conceptualization of such a person would be replete with expectations regarding how he would typically react to certain things or behave in certain circumstances. To understand the subtext of the parable, it is important to understand that the father in the story shattered every stereotype the culture normally associated with such an important person. We'll pay particular attention to those aspects of the father's behavior as we work our way through the parable. But bear in mind that these things were all obvious, unspoken assumptions to Jesus' original audience.

Village life was so deeply ingrained and so clearly understood at every level of that society that the customs reflected in biblical narratives did not usually have to be explained within the narrative. Widely known attitudes did not need to be articulated. Long-standing social customs required no explanation. Nevertheless, these unspoken but culturally understood ideas gave color and meaning to Jesus' stories.

That's why we need to put ourselves (as much as possible) in the same frame of mind as the common people of Jesus' day in order to grasp the significance of His message to them. Also, we must have some fair understanding of their deep-rooted cultural attitudes, the rituals and habits drawn from their religious

Until we begin to comprehend the ideals and attitudes that shaped the culture, we can't expect to gain a full appreciation of the parable's main lesson.

heritage, various social and national traditions, and the distinctive sensibilities of a patriarchal society, especially where people still placed an extremely high value on the stability and stamina of the extended family.

Those are not peripheral or incidental concerns. The cultural context is what brings this parable to life and allows us to live in it. If we are to grasp the true meaning of this classic story in all its spiritual significance, we must go back and try to put ourselves in that very place and time. Until we begin to comprehend the ideals and attitudes that shaped the culture, we can't expect to gain a full appreciation of the parable's main lesson.

BACKGROUND AND SETTING

Luke recorded more parables than any of the other Gospel writers. He alone included a handful of Jesus' longest, most important, most detailed, and most instructive parables, including the good Samaritan (10:29–37), the friend at midnight (11:5–8), the rich fool (12:13–21), the rich man and Lazarus (16:19–31), and the Pharisee and the tax collector (18:9–14). Many of these unique parables are embroidered with the themes of prayer, repentance, forgiveness, justification, and divine grace. The parable of the prodigal son is the magnum opus and centerpiece of these uniquely Lucan parables, weaving together several of those same pivotal themes.

Before examining the actual parable in more detail, let's take note of where it fits in the ministry of Christ and the flow of Luke's Gospel. Jesus had been ministering for nearly three years by this time—preaching that the kingdom of God was at hand and calling men and women to enter the kingdom through repentance and faith in Him (Luke 10:9; 12:31; 18:17).

Jesus was now on His way to Jerusalem during the final months of His earthly life. He was determined to offer Himself as God's perfect sacrifice for sin, die on the cross, and then rise again from the dead, having accomplished the work He must do to gain redemption for sinners. As Luke relates his account of the latter months of Jesus' life, he portrays Jesus as single-mindedly devoted to that one purpose and intent on seeing it to fruition. That becomes a running theme across the second half of Luke, signaled by Luke 9:51: "[Jesus] steadfastly set His face to go to Jerusalem."

At that point, Luke's Gospel takes on a new intonation. Luke repeatedly describes the latter portion of Jesus' ministry as a steadfast journey toward Jerusalem (9:53; 13:22)—even when he is recording geographical movements that took Jesus away from Judea and back toward Galilee (cf. 17:11). Jerusalem became the focal point of Jesus' entire ministry. Luke was too careful a historian and writer for that to be a mistake, and he was too familiar with the geography of the Holy Land to be confused about which direction Jesus needed to travel to get to Jerusalem. Instead, what he was describing was the advancement of Jesus' ministry spiritually, not geographically, as His teaching and His increasingly contentious interactions with the Pharisees brought Him ever closer to His true objective—the cross.

The drama, emotions, and pace in Luke's narrative build inexorably from the end of Luke 9 through the Triumphal Entry (19:28ff). Jesus' own earnest expectancy establishes the tone, epitomized in Luke 12:49–50: "I came to send fire on the earth, and how I wish it were already kindled! But I have a baptism to be baptized with, and how distressed I am till it is accomplished!" Everything Jesus does and says in the second half of Luke's Gospel drives the narrative toward the cross.

The parable of the prodigal son is no exception to that rule. The prominent themes of forgiveness and divine grace reflect the preoccupation of Jesus' own mind and heart. But more ominously, the clear lesson of the parable provided one more significant incident in a long string of public embarrassments that provoked the scribes' and Pharisees' determination to see Him destroyed. According to Luke 11:54, they were already "lying in wait for Him, and seeking to catch Him in something He might say, that they might accuse Him." This parable did not furnish them that opportunity, but it certainly reinforced their motive and hardened their resolve.

SCRIBES AND PHARISEES

As a matter of fact, by chapter 15 of Luke's chronology, the scribes and Pharisees had already become relentless in their pursuit of a reason—*any* reason—to accuse Christ, and that is why they were on the scene in the first place. They were dogging His steps, listening intently to His every word. But they weren't hearing Him with ears of faith, and they weren't following Him because they admired His teaching. Instead, they were stalking Him because they were desperate to find a way to impeach Him—or, better yet, an excuse to kill Him.

The scribes and Pharisees were the chief architects of popular Judaism in that generation. They exercised their influence primarily in the synagogues, where on the weekly Sabbath they taught local assemblies of Jewish people. *Scribes* were professional copiers, editors, and interpreters of the law. They were also the main custodians of the various traditions that governed how the law was applied. Most of the scribes were themselves also Pharisees by conviction (although some of them belonged to a competing sect known as the Sadducees).

The Pharisees were *legalistic*, believing that the way to gain favor with God was by earning merit—and the best way to gain merit in God's eyes, they thought, was through fastidious observance of the Law. The Pharisees' approach to religion naturally fostered self-righteousness (Romans 10:3–4) mixed with overt contempt toward anyone who didn't measure up in their eyes (Luke 18:9).

But the Pharisees were also *hypocritical*. They fastened their hopes chiefly on external and relatively insignificant features of the Law, apparently thinking that the more they stressed the fine points of the Law, the more spiritual they appeared to the people. That's also why they were obsessed with the ceremonial requirements of the Law.

They valued the public display of religion more than private devotion and true righteousness. They would, for instance, make a great show of counting tiny seeds in order to make a tithe (Matthew 23:23). But they neglected the weightier matters of the Law, showing little concern for the moral requirements and moral values, such as justice and mercy and faith (Matthew 23:23). Jesus said they were corrupt inwardly: "You are like whitewashed tombs which indeed appear beautiful outwardly, but inside are full of dead men's bones and all uncleanness. Even so you also outwardly appear righteous to men, but inside you are full of hypocrisy and lawlessness" (vv. 27–28).

PUBLIC ANTAGONISM OF JESUS

Not surprisingly, the scribes and Pharisees were publicly antagonistic to Jesus, and their hostility increased the more they heard Him teach. Of course, since Jesus' doctrine contradicted many of the ideas they stressed in their teaching, any rise in His influence meant a corresponding decline in theirs. Furthermore, the leading scribes and Pharisees (together with leaders of the Sadducees' sect) had brokered a kind of truce with the Roman system, permitting their joint ruling body, known as the Sanhedrin, to retain some semblance of authority over Israel in spiritual and religious matters—even though Rome actually held the political reins. So they were fearful of what Jesus' ascendancy as Israel's Messiah might mean to their spiritual fiefdom. Therefore, "the chief priests and the Pharisees gathered a council and said, 'What shall we do? For this Man works many signs. If we let Him alone like this, everyone will believe in Him, and the Romans will come and take away both our place and nation'" (John 11:47–48).

But don't get the idea that the scribes' and Pharisees' resentment was motivated only by pragmatic concerns about the political implications of Jesus' teaching. Their hatred of Him was also intensely personal, owing mainly to the way He constantly, embarrassingly unmasked their hypocrisy in public. Jesus refused to show artificial respect for their artificial righteousness; instead, He condemned it as *self*-righteousness (Matthew 23:5). He stressed at every opportunity that the pretense of religion the Pharisees had devised was in reality nothing more than a wicked expression of unbelief, and He strictly warned people not to follow their example (v. 3).

The scribes and Pharisees thought of themselves as profound scholars, but Jesus repeatedly castigated them for their ignorance and misunderstanding of the Scriptures, pointedly asking them, "Have you not read . . . ?" (see, for example, Matthew 12:3, 5; 19:4; 22:31; Mark 12:10). Their whole identity was wrapped up in their religion, but Jesus frankly told them they did not even know God (John 8:47). In fact, He called them offspring of the devil (v. 44). He declared they did not know the true way of salvation (John 10:26–27), likening them to snakes and warning them that they were on the road to hell (Matthew 23:33).

> Jesus drew the clearest, most distinct possible line in the sand between His gospel and the Pharisees' self-righteousness. Then He invited all comers to believe in Him and thereby find redemption.

Surely Jesus said all those things to the scribes and Pharisees with profound sorrow and sincere compassion (Luke 19:41–44), but He nevertheless said them plainly. He did not invite the Pharisees to dialogue with Him. He did not seek common ground or congratulate them on whatever points of their doctrine might have already been correct. He did not recruit them to be His cobelligerents in a campaign against the significant moral evils of the day. Instead, Jesus drew the clearest, most distinct possible line in the sand between His gospel and the Pharisees' self-righteousness. Then He invited all comers to believe in Him and thereby find redemption—including people who had been abused and spurned and made into hopeless, lifelong outcasts by the Pharisees' system.

THE POINT OF NO RETURN

Most of the Pharisees hated Jesus for this. Desperate to discredit Him, determined to persuade people that Jesus was not the true Messiah (even against the mountain of evidence His miracles provided to the contrary), the Pharisees publicly declared that Jesus was empowered by the devil himself. They claimed, "This fellow does not cast out demons except by Beelzebub, the ruler of the demons" (Matthew 12:24; cf. Luke 11:15).

That was when the Pharisees' contempt for Jesus literally reached the point of no return. Jesus responded to the charge that His miracles were demonic by showing the irrationality of the argument: "If Satan . . . is divided against himself, how will his kingdom stand?" (Luke 11:18). Then, more ominously, He sounded a dire warning about "the blasphemy against the [Holy] Spirit" (Matthew 12:31), which Jesus described as the one kind of sin for which there can be no forgiveness, ever.

This passage of Scripture is not an easy one to interpret, but as always, the immediate context helps make the meaning clear. Jesus said, "Whoever speaks against the Holy Spirit, it will not be forgiven him, either in this age or in the age to come" (Matthew 12:32). He was not talking about a sin that can be committed out of mere ignorance or inadvertently. Coming after His statement in verse 28, "I cast out demons by the Spirit of God," the definite article in verse 31 ("*the* blasphemy against the Holy Spirit") clearly refers to the deliberately false accusation of the Pharisees. Their bald-faced lie about the source of Jesus' miracles constituted the grossest kind of personal insult to the Spirit of God, who was the real source of those miracles.

This was a sin for which no pardon would ever be available. Again, it was unpardonable not because God's grace was somehow insufficient, but because the attribution of Jesus' miracles to Satan was such a blatant, deliberate, and evil falsehood that if the Pharisees' hearts had not already been utterly and irreparably hardened, they never would have been capable of concocting it in the first place.

Long before this incident, the Pharisees had spurned Christ's many personal pleas for their repentance (Matthew 4:17; Luke 5:32; 13:5). They had rejected every conceivable kind of warning from Him. And they had witnessed His many miracles—undeniable supernatural wonders, not parlor tricks—repeatedly with their own eyes. The Pharisees did not dispute whether actual healings occurred. The signs Jesus performed could not be gainsaid. The Pharisees therefore had ample evidence of His authenticity. They had also marveled at the power, clarity, and authority with which He spoke (Mark 1:22; Luke 4:36). Surely the Pharisees did not *really* believe it was reasonable to write off Jesus' miracles as satanic. But their insistence to the contrary was irrefutable proof of how thoroughly evil their hearts and motives were.

They stood resolutely by that lie, determined to find whatever means they could to prop it up or regain the appearance of their credibility. They tried to shame Jesus because He didn't follow certain man-made traditions that they regarded as essential marks of true piety (Luke 11:37–39). They publicly and relentlessly cross-examined Him about every aspect of His teaching, looking only for ways to incriminate Him (vv. 53–54). They tried to intimidate Him and chase him out of the public arena by reporting rumors about threats Herod had made against His life (13:31). And they criticized Him repeatedly for healing on the Sabbath (13:14; 14:3). In all of this, they thought *they* were the true representatives of God, whom they avowed they knew better than anyone else.

TAX COLLECTORS AND SINNERS

One of the key ways the scribes and Pharisees bolstered their rejection of Jesus was by impugning His character based on whom He associated with. In Luke 14, Jesus unleashes a series of powerful warnings and admonitions (prompted by this annoying preoccupation the Pharisees had with trying to show Him up). Jesus punctuates His discourse with an encouragement to those who (in contrast to the Pharisees) were truly open to spiritual instruction: "He who has ears to hear, let him hear!" (14:35).

At that point, Luke says, "Then all the tax collectors and the sinners drew near to Him *to hear Him*. And the Pharisees and scribes complained, saying, 'This Man receives sinners and eats with them'" (Luke 15:1–2; emphasis added). The Pharisees surely would have resented Jesus' reception of society's outcasts in any case, but their opposition on this occasion was made all the more bitter because of the boldness with which Jesus had repeatedly exposed and condemned their hypocrisy. They no doubt thought this would be a perfect opportunity to embarrass *Him* for a change. If that was their strategy, they could hardly have been more mistaken.

A Friend to Sinners

It is significant that Jesus did not cloister Himself among spiritual people to avoid contact with sinners and lowlifes. When common people, outcasts, and even notorious sinners came to hear Him, He always welcomed them.

A particular scandal stemmed from Jesus' association with tax collectors such as Zacchaeus (Luke 19:1–9) and Matthew (Matthew 19:9). Every true Israelite regarded Rome's occupation of their land as an abomination, and one of the great religious controversies of the day was fought over the question of whether Rome had the right to collect taxes (and especially whether Israelites were obliged to pay those taxes; Matthew 22:15–22). Any Jewish man who accepted a job collecting Roman taxes from his fellow citizens was regarded as a traitor to his country, his religion, and his people. Also, since tax collectors had the power to set fees somewhat arbitrarily, they could get rich by collecting additional fees they did not have to pass on to Rome. Tax collectors were therefore noto-riously corrupt and universally hated. They were utter outcasts, regarded as the very lowest of all sinners. Jesus therefore shocked all of society and especially outraged the religious leaders when He reached out to such people.

What's more, Jesus did not merely associate informally with them from a distance in public settings where He was teaching and they came to listen; He *ate* with them. He sat at their tables and they at His. In the culture of the time, enjoying table fellowship with some-one was a privilege afforded only to friends, family, and one's superi-ors. Respectable people did not eat at the same table with notorious sinners. Dining together was considered tantamount to approval and acceptance.

So to the religious elite of that era, already exasperated by Jesus' failure to give them the kind of public veneration they craved, this looked like the perfect accusation with which they might finally embarrass Him: "He doesn't restrict His fellowship and social involvements to God's people; He is perfectly comfortable with the devil's people, too. He regularly fraternizes with tax collectors, prostitutes and outcasts. Here is ironclad proof that He is satanic: He is a *friend* to sinners" (cf. Matthew 11:19; Luke 7:34).

That was the occasion that triggered the trilogy of parables in Luke 15. The Pharisees seemed very certain that they had the moral high ground now. *They* would never associate with the kinds of people Jesus ate with. They kept away from such people because they believed that was the way to protect their own imag-ined purity.

A Mission to Redeem Sinners

The objection they raised against Christ was actually an echo of a question they had put directly to Christ much earlier in His min-istry: "Why do You eat and drink with tax collectors and sinners?"

(Luke 5:30). Jesus' reply on that occasion should have settled the issue and put them to shame for their wicked attitude. Jesus was by no means a participant in anyone's sin; He was simply taking His ministry to the neediest of sinners. He said, "Those who are well have no need of a physician, but those who are sick. I have not come to call the righteous, but sinners, to repentance" (vv. 31–32).

That last sentence underscores the whole purpose of Jesus' public teaching ministry, and it was a theme he would stress again and again, especially in His conflicts with the Pharisees: He was on a mission to redeem sinners. In fact, the start of public tensions between Jesus and the Pharisees is traceable to that incident in Luke 5. Near the end of His ministry, just prior to His triumphal entry (the event that seemed to spark the culmination of the Pharisees' hostilities), Jesus said practically the same thing again: "The Son of Man has come to seek and to save that which was lost" (Luke 19:10). That simple truth would also be His answer to the Pharisees on this occasion in Luke 15. Only this time, He would answer them with parables.

> Jesus was by no means a participant in anyone's sin; He was simply taking His ministry to the neediest of sinners.

THREE PARABLES WITH A COMMON THEME

The Pharisees' grumbling outrage over Jesus' reception of sinners at this late stage in His ministry clearly revealed how far from the truth they really were. The three parables Jesus told in reply were cleverly designed to illustrate the wicked unreasonableness of the Pharisees' position and to expose their hypocrisy once more for all to see.

Despite the multiple layers and the prolonged length of Jesus' answer to the Pharisees, the substance of His reply is remarkable for its simplicity. Why did He eat with sinners? Because it is the heavenly Father's delight to save lost sinners. The first two parables are brief and uncomplicated, and we'll look at them more closely in the chapter that follows this one. Both parables are about finding what was lost. Both illustrate the lengths to which people will go to find their lost valuables. And the central lesson of both parables is about the natural joy we all experience upon finding what was lost.

> The three parables Jesus told in reply were cleverly designed to illustrate the wicked unreasonableness of the Pharisees' position and to expose their hypocrisy once more for all to see.

The point, of course, was to show that the Pharisees' resentment of Jesus was *unnatural*—perverted, grotesque, and depraved. Their public display of indignation against Him was irrefutable evidence that their own hearts were hopelessly corrupt, and they had no idea what pleased God.

But it was the third parable—the parable of the prodigal son—that struck the point home with the most force. The first two parables depicted great joy in heaven over sinners who repent. The Prodigal Son's story illustrates that heavenly joy too—but then sets it against the background of the elder brother's hellish displeasure over his brother's return and his father's delight.

Jesus unmasks all that ugliness with this moving and beautiful short story. It is, hands down, the greatest five minutes of storytelling ever.

❧ TWO ❧

A Wide-Angle Preview

*The Pharisees and scribes complained, saying, "This Man receives sinners and
eats with them." So He spoke this parable to them . . .*

—Luke 15:2–3

IN CHAPTERS TO COME, WE WILL MEET EACH MAIN CHAR-
acter in the parable of the prodigal son individually, and we will try
to glean as much insight as possible from a careful examination of
how Jesus masterfully developed their roles in this miniature drama.
But as a prelude to that part of our study, and to have a clear perspective on the parable from the outset, let's take a wide-angle look
at the story and its context.

We'll start by asking what the story means. What was the central point Jesus meant to stress in His tale? That may strike some
readers as a backward way of analyzing literature (jumping to the
main point at the very outset), but it's actually a good way of deal-
ing with parables, because, as we already noted in the introduction, it is vital not to lose sight of the main point when you are
reading and interpreting a parable.

Besides, all the major clues about the meaning of this parable
come at the beginning of Luke 15, so if we simply follow the text of
the Gospel account, this is actually the best and most logical place
to start. Our subsequent, closer analysis of later chapters will unfold
the texture and nuances of the parable with much more intricate

19

detail and in a much brighter light. But of course the main point will always remain, and we can stay on track better if we see that point from the beginning and refuse to veer away from it when we delve more carefully into the details of the story.

THE MAIN POINT: JOY IN HEAVEN

As we have already begun to see in the previous chapter, the central lesson of the parable of the prodigal son stands out quite clearly in the context of the passage immediately leading up to and including the parable. Throughout Luke 15, Christ is describing and illustrating the celebratory joy that fills heaven over the repentance of sinners. That is the single, central theme and the major lesson that ties all of Luke 15 together.

Let's remind ourselves that it's vital to see this parable as much as possible through the eyes of someone in the culture of first-century Judaism. To them, the idea that God would freely accept and forgive repentant sinners (including the very worst of them) was a shocking and revolutionary concept. That's why Christ's practice of immediately receiving such people into His fellowship was such a public scandal. Almost no one in that society could conceive of God as reaching out to sinners. Most thought His only attitude toward sinners was stern disapproval, and it was therefore the repentant sinner's duty to work hard to redeem himself and do his best (mainly through legal obedience) to gain whatever degree of divine favor he could earn.

In our culture, the tendency usually goes to the opposite extreme. Too many people today take God's forgiveness for granted. They think of Him as so unconcerned about sin that things such as redemption, atonement, and the wrath of God are unsophisticated, crude, outmoded concepts.

Both perspectives are seriously deficient. God *is* angry over sin (Psalm 7:11), and He *will* punish evildoers with extreme severity

(Isaiah 13:9–13). Scripture is clear about that, and it is a truth we ignore to our own eternal peril. But at the same time, God is "full of compassion, and gracious, longsuffering and abundant in mercy and truth" (Psalm 86:15). He is eager to forgive, and He loves mercy (Exodus 34:6–7; Micah 7:18). More important, His forgiveness is not conditioned on something we do to earn it. He justifies fully and freely because of what Christ has done for sinners. Throughout His earthly life, Christ fulfilled all righteousness (Matthew 3:15; 1 Peter 2:22; Hebrews 7:26), and then He died in the place of those whom He would redeem (1 Corinthians 15:3; 1 John 2:2). Since Christ's righteousness is absolutely perfect and His righteousness is imputed to the believing sinner (2 Corinthians 5:21), each sinner who repents instantly has a perfect standing before God, complete peace with Him, and no fear of future condemnation—all from the very first moment of faith (Romans 3:25–28; 5:1; 8:1). The biblical and theological term used to describe that reality is *justification*. God justifies the ungodly solely through their faith (Romans 4:5).

So without losing sight of the reality of divine wrath against sin, we can celebrate (together with God Himself) the gracious freedom of divine grace, complete forgiveness, and the sinner's full acceptance in the very throne room of heaven. Christ's whole earthly ministry was the living embodiment of that truth, and it went against everything the Pharisees stood for.

> Throughout Luke 15, Christ is describing and illustrating the celebratory joy that fills heaven over the repentance of sinners.

The parable of the prodigal son is the high point and the culmination of Jesus' answer to those Pharisees who were bitter and critical because He received sinners and ate with them. In the Pharisees' jaded perspective, Jesus *consorted* with wicked people, and that was reason enough for righteous people to shun Him. Of course, that accusation (like so much of the Pharisees' teaching) was a dangerous, deadly, demonic lie.

But like most lies, it had enough truth in it to be credible on a superficial level. It was true enough that Jesus was willing to have fellowship with sinners. He constantly showed sinful people sympathy and understanding, even while He was exposing the Pharisees' hypocrisy. To borrow the Pharisees' own words (without the sinister slant they put on it), Jesus was *truly* "a friend of tax collectors and sinners!" (Luke 7:34).

Just a few chapters after the parable of the prodigal son, Luke relates the account of Zacchaeus, a tax collector and notorious sinner (Zacchaeus himself admitted that he had used his position to defraud people; see Luke 19:8). One of the staggering facts of that account is that Jesus invited Himself to stay at Zacchaeus's house in Jericho, and He did it in plain view while throngs of Passover pilgrims were crowding the streets (Luke 19:5). Everyone in polite society would have been appalled to think that a rabbi such as Jesus, a spiritual teacher, would accept the hospitality of a sinful man like Zacchaeus, much less *seek* an affiliation with him.

But there is an important distinction to be made here: Jesus did not consort or seek fellowship with sinners *in their sin*. Scripture describes Him as "holy, harmless, undefiled, *separate* from sinners" (Hebrews 7:26). His overtures to sinners were always in the context of seeking their salvation, offering His grace and mercy, and extending to them forgiveness. He healed them, cleansed them, and released them from the prison of guilt and degradation. Yes, of course Jesus consorted with sinners, but always as their deliverer. He was a true friend of sinners—the most authentic kind of friend. He served them and reached out to them and laid hold of their lives. Jesus didn't affirm them in their sin. Quite the contrary: He gave His whole self for them to redeem them from sin's cruel bondage.

As we have already seen, the Pharisees resented that deeply because they were working hard to cloak their own sin with a show of religiosity. They were convinced of their own moral superiority. But Jesus steadfastly refused to acknowledge or give credence to that pretense. He *always* responded much more positively to the outcasts of society than He did to the typically pompous religious leaders. In fact, He kept insisting that the religious leaders themselves needed to recognize their own sinfulness and their

> Jesus didn't affirm them in their sin. Quite the contrary: He gave His whole self for them to redeem them from sin's cruel bondage.

need of a Savior. That's why even when a leading religious figure like Nicodemus approached him with a friendly overture, His reply was, "You must be born again" (John 3:7).

Nicodemus's case was unusual too. He was a ruling Pharisee (v. 1), but he had an uncharacteristically humble, seeking heart. Even so, Jesus' response to him sounded blunt and abrupt, underscoring Nicodemus's need for a total rebirth—not just a spiritual tune-up, but wholesale conversion. The clear message was a reminder that Pharisees were no less sinners than the people they disparagingly *called* sinners, such as prostitutes, tax collectors, thieves, and other outcasts.

That was Jesus' response to the rare Pharisee whose heart was open. On the other hand, His replies to those who were incorrigibly self-righteous might aptly be described as curt dismissal. Time and again, He would spurn the Pharisees' attitude of superiority with words like these: "Those who are well have no need of a physician, but those who are sick. I have not come to call the righteous, but sinners, to repentance" (Luke 5:31–32).

That's why the Pharisees tried their best to portray Jesus' fellowship with sinners as something unseemly or indecent—as if He were guilty of partaking in the sin itself. Jesus' own words tell us what they were saying about Him: "You say, 'Look, a glutton and a winebibber, a friend of tax collectors and sinners!'" (Luke 7:34). They totally (and deliberately) misrepresented Jesus' involvement in the lives of sinners.

Meanwhile, more and more sinners became disciples of Jesus. These would include people such as Matthew, a former tax collector; and Simon, the converted outlaw and Zealot. As a matter of fact, the disciples closest to Jesus were all former fishermen—working men, not religious scholars. By Peter's own testimony, he was such a sinful man he wasn't worthy to be in the Lord's presence (Luke 5:8). Mary Magdalene had a past sordid enough to include demon possession by seven evil spirits (Luke 8:2). So Jesus' ministry was indeed focused—purposely—among people generally deemed rabble and riffraff.

> Jesus was truly their Friend. The Pharisees had *that* right.

Jesus was truly their Friend. The Pharisees had *that* right.

THE PHARISEES' COMPLAINT: JESUS RECEIVES SINNERS

As we began to see in chapter 1, this issue had become a major and recurring theme in Jesus' conflicts with the Pharisees. It was one of a handful of complaints they kept bringing up against Him, until their objections to His ministry virtually became a predictable threefold refrain: "He violates the Sabbath" (Luke 6:2, 6–11; 13:14; 14:3–6); "He claims too much for Himself" (John 5:18; 8:54–58; 10:30–33); and "He fraternizes with lowlifes" (Matthew 9:10–11; 11:19).

The latter part of that refrain is what touched off the long discourse that begins with the three parables of Luke 15. Notice that Luke says, "Then all the tax collectors and the sinners drew near to Him to hear Him" (Luke 15:1). They came on their own initiative. Furthermore, it was Jesus' *teaching* that appealed to them. They wanted to hear this amazing Man who claimed (and miraculously demonstrated) that He had power and authority to forgive sins (Luke 5:21–24; 7:48). The gospel message—with its promise of new life, full pardon, and spiritual cleansing—drew to Jesus those who were fed up with sin.

There must surely have been a wonderful spirit of joy and festivity constantly surrounding Jesus. But it was not the kind of wild party atmosphere the Pharisees described. It was the pure, heavenly joy of salvation. It was the heartfelt rejoicing of liberated captives—men and women who formerly lived as abject slaves under a spiritual death sentence, now delivered into glorious freedom and eternal life. It was a constant, unspeakable joy. It was a deep gladness that transcends heaven and earth—and spans time and eternity. It was certainly nothing like the staid, dour, and pretentious dignity of formal religiosity.

The religious power-mongers did not like this. Luke 15:2 says, "The Pharisees and scribes *complained*, saying, 'This Man receives sinners and eats with them.'" The Greek verb is emphatic, meaning that they murmured passionately and persistently—no doubt secretly diffusing their bitter complaint throughout the multitudes like gossip.

THE INFLUENCE OF THE SCRIBES AND PHARISEES

Much evidence in the Gospel accounts suggests that the scribes' and Pharisees' constant opposition and complaining actually *did* dissuade many people from following Jesus. After one public confontation with the Pharisees in John 6, verse 66 says, "From that time many of His disciples went back and walked with Him no more." The Pharisees also nearly succeeded in provoking a public stoning of Christ in John 8:59. In effect, by stirring up the multitudes against Christ, they were turning people away from the kingdom of God, closing the door, and barring it to everyone—and Jesus expressly condemned them for that. In Matthew 23:13, He pronounced this formal curse on them: "But woe to you, scribes and Pharisees, hypocrites! For you shut up the kingdom of heaven against men; for you neither go in yourselves, nor do you allow those who are entering to go in" (cf. Luke 11:52).

It's easy to see why people in that culture would be seriously conflicted when they heard about the Pharisees' opposition. After all, they had been taught from childhood to regard the scribes and Pharisees as their main spiritual mentors and the nation's leading religious experts. The Pharisees' open hatred of Christ therefore spread like a cancer. And the more Jesus' teaching dealt with difficult or challenging themes, the more people became either hostile or indifferent to Jesus.

> The more Jesus' teaching dealt with difficult or challenging themes, the more people became either hostile or indifferent to Jesus.

John 6 shows how and why the vast majority of people finally turned away from Christ—and many even turned completely against Him. The multitudes followed Him as long as He was feeding them and doing other miraculous works, but they did not like His strong teaching. As a matter of fact, Luke 14:26–35, the passage immediately preceding the exchange in Luke 15, includes some of Jesus' most strongly worded teaching. It's all about denying self, hating father and mother, and counting the cost of discipleship.

Ironically, just when the self-satisfied, respectable, materialistic multitudes began to drift away because of that kind of teaching, that's when Luke says the tax collectors and sinners drew near. (That, by the way, is a damning commentary on today's popular strategies for reaching the rebellious, disenfranchised, and outcasts of society by softening the gospel and stressing only its positive elements. It likewise exposes the folly of appealing to unbelievers who are already comfortable in some false religion by looking for points of agreement with them.)

Nevertheless, the Pharisees' conspiracy to oppose Jesus *did* ultimately bring about precisely the result they hoped for. Within six months, some of the very same common people who once "heard Him gladly" (Mark 12:37) would be screaming for His blood.

JESUS RESPONDS WITH THREE PARABLES

Of course, Jesus saw clearly what was happening, so He answered the matter rather definitively with a trio of parables.

Since the parables of Luke 15 all make exactly the same point and the first two are very brief, it might be helpful to examine the first two parables as a short prelude to the parable of the prodigal son. It is with the parable of the prodigal son that Jesus scores the really hard polemical body blows—and in the end, the knockout punch—against the hypocrisy and wickedness of the scribes and Pharisees. But the first two parables set up that sparring with a couple of comparatively mild-looking jabs.

The Lost Sheep

The first parable paints a very simple, familiar, pastoral image.

> What man of you, having a hundred sheep, if he loses one of them, does not leave the ninety-nine in the wilderness, and go after the one which is lost until he finds it? And when he has found it, he lays it on his shoulders, rejoicing. And when he comes home, he calls together his friends and neighbors, saying to them, "Rejoice with me, for I have found my sheep which was lost!" I say to you that likewise there will be more joy in heaven over one sinner who repents than over ninety-nine just persons who need no repentance. (vv. 4–7)

Sheep were so common in that culture that virtually all Jesus' hearers immediately would have tuned into the imagery. Here was a shepherd missing one sheep out of a flock of a hundred. What should he do?

Everyone knew the answer. Sheep are not generally independent thinkers. Their natural inclination is to stay together in flocks. If one got lost, it was usually owing to the animal's sheer stupidity or bumbling clumsiness. Perhaps the lost sheep got itself on a ledge where it couldn't get off or somehow didn't notice when the rest of the flock wandered away.

Either way, the lost sheep was in mortal danger. A sheep separated from the flock and left to wander by itself in the wilderness *will* die, even with an abundance of food and water all around. It's only a matter of time before the lost sheep would succumb to the stress of being separated from the flock, the threat of predators, or exposure to the elements. Any or all of those could be fatal in short order.

So the shepherd's duty would be to leave his flock in a safe place together and go in search of the lost sheep. He would search diligently for the wayward lamb, and when he found it, he would joyfully bring it home.

There's an image of compassion and an illustration of divine grace in the way the shepherd "lays it on his shoulders" and brings it home. He doesn't beat or berate the wandering sheep. He doesn't even leave it to the sheep to travel home in his own power. He lifts it up and carries it, and he does so with joy and delight rather than anger or exasperation. In fact, in Jesus' account, the shepherd is so delighted over the return of the sheep that he calls together his friends and neighbors to celebrate.

This kind of celebration perfectly pictures the overflowing joy that characterized Jesus' earthly ministry to sinners. It is a joy that cannot be contained. It's also contagious. Who would not want to join such a celebration?

What's most amazing about the parable, however, is that Jesus was not merely drawing a parallel between the joyful shepherd and the joy that attended His earthly ministry. He expressly said that the parable pictures *heaven's* joy: "Likewise there will be more joy in heaven over one sinner who repents than over ninety-nine just persons who need no repentance" (v. 7). Here's the point: that celebratory joy that constantly surrounded Jesus' dealings with sinners—the same spirit of jubilation the Pharisees so bitterly resented and tried to characterize as unrighteous revelry—is the very same atmosphere you'll find in heaven every time a sinner repents. It is actually the joy of God Himself.

In fact, Jesus said, God's joy over the redemption of a single sinner is a far *greater* joy than there would be if ninety-nine righteous people could be found "who need no repentance" (Luke 15:7). Of course, no such persons really exist, but that's how the Pharisees tended to think of themselves. Before finishing this chapter, we'll answer the question of whom Jesus was referring to when He spoke of "just persons who need no repentance." But the point Jesus was making here starts with God's attitude toward *penitent* sinners.

The parable of the lost sheep painted an amazing, mind-blowing picture for most of Jesus' hearers. They knew (much better than the average person does today) how much God hates sin. They understood (in a way the postmodern mind has deliberately forgotten) that "God is a just judge, and God is angry with the wicked every day" (Psalm 7:11). They had a clear understanding of God's righteous wrath against evil.

> Jesus' ministry embodied a truth that was beyond most people's comprehension: God welcomes repentant sinners with undiluted joy and gladness.

But Jesus' ministry embodied a truth that was beyond most

people's comprehension: God welcomes repentant sinners with undiluted joy and gladness. He doesn't respond to the sinner's penitence with chiding, disgust, or angry demands for retribution. He receives sinners gladly.

In fact, far from punishing the returning sinner or demanding some kind of penance or self-atonement to pay for those past sins, the Savior throws a heavenly party in the returning sinner's honor. Just like the shepherd did in Jesus' parable.

By the way, one of the earliest symbols of Christian art—even before the cross was adopted as the main symbol of Christianity— was the image of a shepherd carrying a sheep home on the back of his neck with the sheep's legs coming down across his shoulders. It was an echo of the famous Old Testament imagery that anticipated Israel's Messiah: "He will feed His flock like a shepherd; He will gather the lambs with His arm, and carry them in His bosom, and gently lead those who are with young" (Isaiah 40:11).

So here's a perfect picture of divine grace: the shepherd in this short parable does *all* the work. He seeks and finds the lost lamb, and then he carries it home on his shoulders. Having done that, he is so overflowing with joy and jubilation that only a public celebration will do to express them.

The second parable makes the very same point.

The Lost Coin

Without pausing for a response to His first parable, Jesus segues into His second illustration.

> Or what woman, having ten silver coins, if she loses one coin, does not light a lamp, sweep the house, and search carefully until she finds it? And when she has found it, she calls her friends and neighbors together, saying, "Rejoice with me, for I have found the piece which I lost!" Likewise, I say to you, there is joy in the presence of the angels of God over one sinner who repents. (Luke 15:8–10)

The plot and lesson are virtually identical to the first parable. Only the setting and the main character have changed. Now it's a woman in possession of ten valuable coins, but she loses one. So eager is she to find that one missing coin that she lights an oil lamp (so that she can see into every dark corner) and sweeps out her whole house (so that her search doesn't miss an inch, including what's under the furniture). The emphasis here is on the thoroughness and persistence of her search. She searches "carefully until she finds it" (v. 8).

Then the woman—just like the shepherd in the first parable—is so delighted to recover what was lost that she shares the good tidings with all her friends and neighbors. Again, the lesson is about her joy—overflowing happiness. She was overtaken by a delight so rich and wonderful that she *had* to share it with everyone she knew.

In these two parables, Jesus used imagery that is easy to relate to. Who doesn't know the joy of finding a prized possession that has been lost? These are real-life scenarios that we can easily relate to, even in our contemporary cultural context.

> Heaven's joy over the redemption of sinners is an ecstatic, euphoric, over-the-top kind of exultation.

The only feature of those two stories that seems exaggerated is the celebration. Most people who find a lost coin or a lost animal wouldn't actually go to the trouble of calling friends and neighbors together and having a public gala to rejoice. But for someone actually to take the step of calling friends and neighbors together to share in the festivities, that person's sense of exhilaration would have to be profound indeed.

And that was precisely Jesus' point. Heaven's joy over the redemption of sinners is an ecstatic, euphoric, over-the-top kind of exultation.

That, in fact, is God's own response whenever a sinner is converted. Notice that Jesus doesn't speak of the "joy *of* the angels" but "joy *in the presence of* the angels" (v. 10) and "joy in heaven" (v. 7). It's the joy of the Savior Himself. Like the shepherd who found the sheep and the woman who found the coin, the Good Shepherd wishes to share His great joy over the salvation of sinners with anyone and everyone who will rejoice with Him.

OPPOSITION HERE ON EARTH

The Pharisees' resentment, therefore, was an insult to God. It was blasphemy of the highest order. Jesus made *that* point by introducing them to the Prodigal Son. The elder brother in this tale symbolizes the Pharisees. His resentment, which contrasts starkly with the father's joy, was an exact mirror of the Pharisees' mentality.

One reason Jesus often used parables was to conceal truths from unbelievers (Luke 8:10). But the parable of the prodigal son, as we will see, painted the ugliness of the Pharisees' attitude with such vivid realism that no one could possibly miss the point.

> The parable of the prodigal son, as we will see, painted the ugliness of the Pharisees' attitude with such vivid realism that no one could possibly miss the point.

The parable of the prodigal son continues with the same theme as the two earlier parables, and it has a very similar plot. We have heard about the recovery of a lost sheep and a lost coin. Now here is the recovery of a lost son. In each parable, something lost is found, and that is followed by a great celebration.

The central imagery is parallel in all three parables. Each parable illustrates the joy of God over the recovery of a lost sinner. Each parable also has a figure representing

Christ, whose mission is to seek and to save the lost. In the first parable, the shepherd is symbolic of Christ; in the second, the woman takes that role; and in the Prodigal Son's story, it's the father. (Bear that fact in mind. It is common to assume that the Prodigal's father represents the heavenly Father, but the parallelism of these three stories suggests that he is actually a symbol of Christ. The full significance of that point will become clear in the Epilogue.)

A handful of notable distinctives mark this parable. First, this is the only one of the three parables where the Christ figure is not shown actively searching and seeking. (His seeking is strongly hinted at by the fact that the father saw the Prodigal returning "when he was still a great way off".) But the perspective here is different. The first two stories emphasize Christ's role as the seeker—the one who finds and rejoices. But the third story looks at conversion from the sinner's perspective, highlighting the Prodigal's rejection, ruin, repentance, and recovery.

> It is common to assume that the Prodigal's father represents the heavenly Father, but the parallelism of these three stories suggests that he is actually a symbol of Christ.

In fact, that's another unique feature of this parable. It's the only one of the three that illustrates the sinner's repentance. But it does so with a wonderful thoroughness, giving us perhaps the finest example in the New Testament of what true repentance looks like.

Still, the most obvious and significant difference between this parable and its two immediate predecessors is the shocking plot turn that takes place just when we think the story is over. The Prodigal returns. The father hosts a great celebration. That's where the two earlier stories ended—when that which was lost has been found.

But this story continues, and we meet the character who symbolizes the scribes and Pharisees: the Prodigal's elder brother. He comes on the scene, resentful of the celebration, critical of the father's joy, so entirely focused on himself and his accomplishments that he is utterly unable to rejoice with the father over the return of his lost brother. The elder brother's attitude stands in stark contrast to the joy that was the central feature in all three parables up to this point. Here is the counterpoint Jesus was building to all along. This parable is a rebuke of the attitude of the religious leaders who resented His ministry, which was done for the joy of God.

> This parable is a rebuke of the attitude of the religious leaders who resented His ministry, which was done for the joy of God.

If you can imagine how the scribes and Pharisees would have heard these parables, the point is powerful indeed. Up to the vital turning point where Jesus introduces the father's staggering forgiveness, they could well have listened sympathetically to all three parables, nodding their heads in agreement. Who doesn't understand the joy of finding what was lost? Religious leaders could relate to those stories as easily as anyone else. Christ's imagery would have drawn them in. They could listen with interest and a degree of understanding. They fancied themselves ethicists with high values, and the ethics in these stories were rather straightforward and noncontroversial.

The *theology* of these stories, however, was somewhat veiled—until the elder brother appeared. Then it became clear that the parable was designed to show their bitter contempt for sinners in its true light. Jesus was exposing the error of the Pharisees' own self-righteous superiority complex by contrasting their contempt for sinners with the spirit of divine compassion that permeated His whole earthly ministry. He began the parable by laying out an ethical principle the Pharisees would naturally give assent to, and then He used it like a knife to dissect the serious deficiencies in their theology, their perception of God, and their attitude toward other people. The ugliness of the Pharisees' hypocrisy and self-righteousness were thus laid open for all to see. This was yet another devastating public humiliation for them.

Incidentally, the reference in Luke 15:7 to "persons who need no repentance" was a reference to the Pharisees. Jesus was not suggesting that they were truly righteous or that they really had no need for repentance. Just the opposite. But the phrase describes how the Pharisees saw themselves. Christ often rebuked them for this attitude. In Luke 5:32, He told them, "Those who are well have no need of a physician, but those who are sick. I have not come to call the righteous, but sinners, to repentance." That was meant as a stern reprimand and repudiation of their arrogant attitude; He was not suggesting that they were really doing just fine on their own.

In Luke 18:9, Jesus "spoke [a] parable to some who trusted in themselves that they were righteous, and despised others." It was a parable about a Pharisee and a publican (a Jewish tax collector for the Roman government), in which the Pharisee looks askance at a repenting publican and has the audacity to thank God that he, the Pharisee, isn't such a bad sinner. That was the typical Pharisee's perspective.

> Jesus told the parable of the prodigal son primarily for the Pharisees' benefit and as a rebuke to them.

In fact, immediately after Luke concludes his account of the string of parables that began with the lost sheep, he records that Jesus rebuked the Pharisees plainly, in a way that summed up the main point of the parables: "You are those who justify yourselves before men, but God knows your hearts. For what is highly esteemed among men is an abomination in the sight of God" (Luke 16:15).

That is the big-picture meaning of what is going on in this parable. Jesus told the parable of the prodigal son primarily for the Pharisees' benefit and as a rebuke to them.

A POINT LEFT UNSPOKEN: TRUE REDEMPTION IN CHRIST

The parable nevertheless contains a message and an application that every one of us must heed. It wouldn't do for us to make the same mistake as the Pharisees. Scripture doesn't give us room to stand in the distance, looking disparagingly at the Pharisees and thanking God we're not like *them*.

In fact, one of the clear implications of the story is that *no one* is free from the need for repentance. If the Pharisees needed to repent, despite their obsession with the minute details of the ceremonial law, how much more do we need to repent for not taking the holiness of God as seriously as we should?

Notice that Jesus did not rebuke the Pharisees for counting out little seeds to tithe; He rebuked them for using that kind of thing as a cloak to hide their failure with regard to the more important *moral* aspects of the Law. He told them, "You pay tithe of mint and anise and cummin, and have neglected the weightier matters of the law: justice and mercy and faith. *These you ought to have done, without leaving the others undone*" (Matthew 23:23; emphasis added).

If you can hear the parable of the prodigal son and not identify yourself, you are missing the unspoken point of Jesus' message. It is a call to repentance, and it applies to prodigals (immoral, outcast sinners) and Pharisees (moral, respectable hypocrites) alike. Both the point and the counterpoint of the parable underscore this idea. On the one hand, we see how repentance unleashes heaven's joy. On the other hand, we learn that refusing to see one's own need for repentance is nothing but stubborn, self-righteous opposition to heaven's agenda. Therefore, the parable demands repentance from prodigals and Pharisees.

The promise of redemption for penitent sinners goes hand in hand with that truth. There's an unspoken but wholly gracious plea contained in these vivid images of profound joy in heaven whenever that which was lost is recovered. It reminds us of Jesus' tender words in John 6:37: "The one who comes to Me I will by no means cast out."

A PERSONAL APPLICATION:
DON'T WAIT UNTIL IT'S TOO LATE!

As we begin a more detailed study of the parable, its plot, and its characters, I encourage you to use your reading of this book as an opportunity to do some serious, heartfelt self-examination. If you're new to the Christian faith, the parable of the prodigal son is an excellent starting place for studying God's Word and learning to apply its truths to your life. Even if you have been a church member for years, you will benefit greatly from the exercise.

One of the important lessons we will learn from the negative example of the elder brother and the hard-shelled self-righteousness of the Pharisees is that it is possible to spend an entire lifetime in and around the household of faith, giving every appearance of diligent work and faithful service—and yet to be totally out of harmony with heaven's joy. If there's any possibility that is your condition, dear reader, do not wait to discover it until it is too late to apply the remedy.

PART 2

The Prodigal

~

A certain man had two sons. And the younger of them said to his father, "Father, give me the portion of goods that falls to me." So he divided to them his livelihood. And not many days after, the younger son gathered all together, journeyed to a far country, and there wasted his possessions with prodigal living. But when he had spent all, there arose a severe famine in that land, and he began to be in want. Then he went and joined himself to a citizen of that country, and he sent him into his fields to feed swine. And he would gladly have filled his stomach with the pods that the swine ate, and no one gave him anything. But when he came to himself, he said, "How many of my father's hired servants have bread enough and to spare, and I perish with hunger! I will arise and go to my father, and will say to him, 'Father, I have sinned against heaven and before you, and I am no longer worthy to be called your son. Make me like one of your hired servants.'" And he arose and came to his father.

—Luke 15:11–20

❦ THREE ❧

His Shameless Demand

The younger [Son] said to his father, "Father, give me the portion of goods that falls to me."

—Luke 15:12

WE'RE READY NOW TO WORK THROUGH THE PARABLE of the prodigal son with careful attention to the characters, the plot, and the details Jesus highlighted in the narrative.

Jesus introduces the main characters in the first verse: "A certain man had two sons" (Luke 15:11). As the story unfolds, the focus shifts from one character to another. The younger son—the Prodigal—is the main focus at the start (vv. 12–20). But then midway through the story, the father takes center stage (vv. 20–24), followed by the elder brother (vv. 25–31). The parable naturally divides into those three sections, and as Jesus develops the tale, with each shift in focus, the plot takes a surprising turn. The typical first-time hearer's train of thought and expectations are therefore jolted with each successive shift in the story line.

As the parable begins, the younger son appears to be cast in the scoundrel's role as the central character. In the closing section, however, the *elder* brother is unmasked as the real villain. As the focus of the story turns to the elder brother, we learn the main lesson of the parable from his negative example.

Some have even suggested that a better name for the parable

41

would be "The Self-Righteous Big Brother," or something similar. Others have proposed titles focusing on the father's mercy and forgiveness ("The Parable of the Forgiving Father," and so on). But it's hard to think of any title that would do justice to the full sweep of truth Jesus lays out in this short tale.

> The Prodigal Son is an object lesson about true repentance.

The three-part form of this parable is deliberate and ingenious. It highlights in quick succession three important ideas, all closely related to the central theme of Luke 15: heaven's joy when a sinner repents. The Prodigal Son is an object lesson about true repentance. The father personifies the joy of heaven. And the embittered elder brother stands in stark contrast to both of those ideas. He is the embodiment of the Pharisees' pretentious self-righteousness and its natural byproduct—ungodly resentment over the grace and goodness of God to others.

We'll begin, as Jesus did, by focusing on the younger brother—the Prodigal Son himself.

The derivation of that name is worth pausing to notice. The word *prodigal* doesn't appear in the King James Version. It's a very old English word that speaks of reckless wastefulness or lavish extravagance. It has virtually fallen out of usage in modern English, except in reference to this parable. It is sometimes used in reference to wayward sons

> The main idea behind the word *prodigal* is that of wastefulness, immoderation, excess, and dissipation.

and daughters. But it doesn't speak of youthful rebellion or truancy per se. The main idea behind the word *prodigal* is that of wastefulness, immoderation, excess, and dissipation.

The word *is* used in Luke 15:13 in the New King James Version, where we are told this younger brother "wasted his possessions with prodigal living." The Greek term there is *asôtôs*, meaning wastefulness—but don't get the notion that the Prodigal's dominant character flaw was merely that he was a spendthrift. As we'll soon see, the Greek expression is much stronger than that, conveying strong overtones of licentiousness, promiscuity, and moral debauchery.

The young man is a classic illustration of an undisciplined young person who wastes the best part of his life through extravagant self-indulgence and becomes a slave to his own lust and sin. He is a living picture of the course of sin and how it inevitably debases the sinner.

THE REBEL'S ASTONISHING INSOLENCE

Just the introduction to Jesus' tale was probably enough to elicit a gasp from the scribes and Pharisees: "The younger [son] said to his father, 'Father, give me the portion of goods that falls to me'" (vv. 11–12). The young man's request, as Jesus described it, was outrageous, impudent, and grossly dishonoring to the father.

> Everything about the demand the boy made cut against the grain of Hebrew society's core values.

The picture Jesus paints is of a young man, who is apparently not yet married—because he wants to go and sow his wild oats. He was probably in his teens and obviously filled with shameless disrespect toward his father. His request for an early inheritance reveals how passionately deep-seated and wickedly hard-hearted his defiance was. Anyone acquainted with Middle Eastern culture would instantly see this (and most would find it repugnant in the extreme) because everything about the demand the boy made cut against the grain of Hebrew society's core values.

Disregard for His Inheritance

To begin with, the younger son's attitude regarding his inheritance was entirely inappropriate. From the earliest days of Israel, the laws governing the passage of family estates from generation to generation were among the most important and most distinctive cultural principles codified in the law of Moses. Family lands and possessions were not to be sold or transferred out of the family line. In dire cases where land *had* to be sold to avoid a disastrous bankruptcy, the Law even had a provision that guaranteed the eventual return of that property to its rightful family during the year of Jubilee (Leviticus 25:23–34).

The duty of keeping one's legacy intact was well understood by all. This is seen in Naboth's indignation when Ahab wanted to purchase his family's land to turn it into a garden adjacent to the royal palace. Naboth said, "The LORD forbid that I should give the inheritance of my fathers to you!" (1 Kings 21:3). That perspective was deeply ingrained in Israel's value system, going all the way back to when "Abraham gave all that he had to Isaac" (Genesis 25:5).

A principle known as *the law of primogeniture* governed the transfer of a family's inheritance in Israel. It meant the firstborn son would receive a double portion of the family legacy. On rare and extraordinary occasions, the double portion could be given to a younger son instead—such as when Isaac rather than Ishmael became Abraham's sole heir, or when Jacob got the birthright from Esau. But normally the birthright went to the eldest son.

Deuteronomy 21:15–17 recognizes the legitimacy and importance of this practice. (That text forbids the transfer of the birthright to a younger sibling for reasons stemming from sinful favoritism.) The birthright included not only that extra measure of wealth but also the responsibility of family headship over whoever remained in the immediate household when the father died. The greater part of a family's land and possessions—and the nucleus of the family itself—was thus kept intact from generation to generation.

Younger sons were by no means disenfranchised. They received a fair share of the inheritance too. In an important sense, they benefited greatly from the economic principles established by the law of primogeniture. Rather than mercilessly subdividing a family's property and assets every generation (or taxing everyone's inheritance into oblivion), the practice gave firstborn sons a better financial foundation to build on and thereby established a stronger family core. That, in turn, provided support and stability for younger sons as well. The system was designed to increase wealth all around.

It is patently obvious that the younger son in Jesus' parable had not an ounce of gratitude in his heart for the legacy that generations of his family had provided for his father—and one day for him. He lacked both patience and discipline. Worst of all, by all appearances, he lacked any authentic love for his father.

Dishonor for His Father

This was perhaps the most disturbing aspect of the Prodigal Son's behavior. For a son in that culture to request his inheritance early was tantamount to saying, "Dad, I wish you were dead. You are in the way of my plans. You are a barrier. I want my freedom. I want my fulfillment. And I want out of this family now. I have other plans that don't involve you; they don't involve this family; they don't involve this estate; they don't even involve this village. I want nothing to do with any of you. Give me my inheritance now, and I am out of here."

> For a son in that culture to request his inheritance early was tantamount to saying, "Dad, I wish you were dead."

In a culture where honor was so important and the fifth commandment ("Honor your father and your mother") was a governing law, this young man's impertinence was worse than merely scandalous. Any son who made such a breathtakingly inappropriate request from a healthy father would have been regarded as the lowest form of miscreant. It was not his prerogative to demand his inheritance early. Not only was he implying that he wished his father were dead; he was in effect purposely committing a kind of symbolic filial suicide. Any son who made such a brazen demand could expect to be written off as dead by his father. Evidently that mattered little to this reckless son. In fact, that would give him the freedom he craved. If he managed to get the early inheritance to boot, so much the better.

Incidentally, in that culture, the normal response to this level of impudence would be, at the very minimum, a hard slap across the face from the father. This would typically be done publicly to shame the son who had showed such disdain for his father. (If that seems too severe, bear in mind that the law of Moses prescribed death by stoning for incorrigibly rebellious children [Deuteronomy 21:18–21].) So a son guilty of dishonoring his father to this degree could well expect to be dispossessed of everything he had and then permanently dismissed from the family. Reckoned as dead. That's how serious this breach was. As a matter of fact, that is reflected when the Prodigal comes back and the father says, "This my son was dead" (v. 24). The father says it again to the older brother: "Your brother was dead" (v. 32). It was not uncommon in that time and place to hold an actual funeral for a child who insolently abandoned home and family in this way. Even today in strict Jewish families, parents will sometimes say "kaddish" (the formal recitation of a funeral prayer) over a son or daughter who is disowned for this kind of behavior.

Once disowned by a father, there was almost no way for a rebellious child to come back and regain his position in the family. If wanted back at all, he must make restitution for whatever dishonor he caused the family and for whatever possessions he might have taken when he ran away. Even then, he might expect to forfeit many of the rights that he previously enjoyed as a family member. He could certainly forget about receiving any further inheritance.

The lines of family honor were clear to everyone in society. The father was at the head of the list, usually with the mother at his side. Next in order of honor came the eldest brother, with younger siblings at the bottom of the pecking order.

So in Jesus' parable, the hierarchy is obvious. The father, as the family patriarch, is to be highly honored. No mother is in evidence, so the father may have been a widower, which would mean the father and two sons were the nucleus of this household, with servants who showed them honor.

However, the younger son would be expected to honor not only the father but the elder brother as well. He might well have resented his position in the family, thinking he was not much better off than the household servants.

> The son was either oblivious to his own shame or totally unconcerned about it. So what if his behavior brought dishonor on the whole family?

Whatever was going on in his mind, the son was either oblivious to his own shame or totally unconcerned about it. So what if his behavior brought dishonor on the whole family? As soon as he had his inheritance, he would leave home and family and country behind and travel into a far country where no one knew him anyway. Then he would be free at last to do whatever he wanted.

Jesus could hardly have painted a scenario that would portray greater shame. Given the social structure of Israel, this was the very lowest a son could go.

Demand for His Birthright

The way the Prodigal made his demand was calloused and cold-hearted: "Father, give me the portion of goods that falls to me" (Luke 15:12).

The Greek expression translated "portion of goods" is found nowhere else in Scripture. It's not the normal Greek word for *inheritance*. It's not a term that would normally be applied to real estate, fixed assets, or anything permanently situated on the family property. Instead, it's a word that speaks of personal valuables—especially movable property and liquid assets. It literally means "my share of the family's belongings." He was demanding that his father's household goods, personal valuables, and miscellaneous material possessions be inventoried and distributed early.

That suggestion was, of course, as impractical as it was audacious. In any two-son family following the law of primogeniture, one-third of all family assets would go to the younger son *when the father died*. To demand a third of the household goods while the father was still living was both absurd and unreasonable.

It's doubtful that the Prodigal really expected his father to meet such a demand. No matter. He would happily accept payment in coins or bank notes. He was undoubtedly willing to settle for far less than the fair market value of his actual inheritance. Plainly, his only plan was to take whatever he could get his hands on and leave home as soon as possible. He was not interested in any part of the long-term family legacy. A share in the family's property and livestock would only tie him down. He was basically asking to be cashed out.

In effect, the Prodigal Son was offering to sell his birthright for whatever money his father had on hand. That would probably be a considerable amount by any measure. This was clearly a prosperous family. They had hired servants (Luke 15:19, 22). The father was affluent enough to hire musicians and dancers for an impromptu celebration (v. 25). They owned livestock, including a fattened calf readily available for their own use at a moment's notice—which was the kind of luxury only a very wealthy family could afford.

Of course, this young man knew he would eventually come into a substantial inheritance, but he was fed up with waiting for it. He wanted whatever he could get *now*, chiefly because he needed it to finance his rebellion. He didn't want any of the responsibility that came with the inheritance. He wanted no part in the ongoing management of the estate. In fact, what he seems to have wanted most of all was to get rid of the duties, the expectations, and the stewardship that came with being the son of such a successful man.

> In effect, the Prodigal Son was offering to sell his birthright for whatever money his father had on hand.

In essence, he was telling his father, "All I want is a fair share of the family assets, and I'll get out of your life. I'm not asking for your advice; I just want my portion of what's coming to me. I don't want to be led, and I certainly don't want to be a leader. I don't need accountability, and I don't need you."

Like every unruly adolescent, the Prodigal was clearly miserable. He thought what he needed was more independence. He was tired of the cultural pressure to honor his father. He certainly couldn't see any benefit to letting his father's viewpoint and values govern his life any longer. He was determined to remove himself as far as possible from every obligation, to cast off all restraint, and *especially* to remove himself from his father's authority.

It was, of course, any father's prerogative to give gifts to his children. And it was not unheard of in the Jewish culture at that time for a father to assign specific portions of the family estate to individual heirs long before he died. He might say, for example, regarding a particular portion of land or a treasured possession, "That is yours. It's part of the two-thirds you'll receive as my firstborn son." Or, "Here is something I want you to have. It's part of the one-third you're going to get as my younger son."

But even if a father did distribute his estate early, the sons weren't permitted to take full and independent possession of their inheritance until the father died. In that culture, where honor was so important, every father was expected to remain ultimately in charge and finally responsible for the entire household and all its assets until he died. The father (if he were truly honorable) could *never* relinquish his duty as head of the family. Such a thing was precluded by a host of traditions that were tied to the fifth commandment: "Honor your father and your mother" (Exodus 20:12).

In fact, the Mishnah (a compendium of traditions governing how the Law was interpreted) mandated that if a father distributed his estate early, the sons had to hold the property until he died. The sons might manage an asset or cultivate a plot of land as if it were already their own. But the father maintained a kind of de facto ownership. He still had the dominant voice in decisions about family affairs. He still oversaw how they managed the property. And he still had a right to share in any income that was produced. Only after the father's death could sons do with their inheritance whatever they pleased. In other words, an early inheritance, though a wonderful benefit, did not release a son completely from his father's authority.

> The Prodigal was not asking for *that* kind of gift. He was demanding a way out of the family.

But the Prodigal was not asking for *that* kind of gift. He was demanding a way out of the family.

THE FATHER'S SURPRISING RESPONSE

In the village life of that time, everyone knew everyone else's business. Besides, the Prodigal's plan to leave home guaranteed that his rebellion would in short order become public knowledge and grist for the village rumor mill. This thoughtless rebel was blithely erecting a mountain of dishonor over his father, his family, and his own reputation.

Sadly for the father, there was nothing he could do to cover or remove the shame, short of publicly disowning the boy. That is no doubt precisely what others in the village would expect and possibly even urge the father to do. Any self-respecting father in that culture would naturally feel he *had* to disgrace the son as publicly as possible—giving him the ceremonial slap across the face, a public denunciation, formal dismissal from the family, and possibly even a funeral. After all, it was the only way to avoid allowing the boy to bring a lasting reproach against the family's good name.

> Sadly for the father, there was nothing he could do to cover or remove the shame, short of publicly disowning the boy.

Division of His Livelihood

Instead, the father "divided to them his livelihood" (v. 12). Rather than publicly strike the boy across the face for his insolence, this father granted his rebel son exactly what he asked for.

Here is where Jesus' story would have elicited a second great gasp from the scribes and Pharisees. If the father had divided his estate between his sons out of his own will and gracious generosity, then it would be understood and perhaps even admired. But to honor an impudent request from a defiant youth in this way was unheard of—especially since this course of action quite literally cost the father everything he had.

Most of Jesus' listeners—particularly the Pharisees—would see this as a shameful act by the father. By the standards of that culture, it was a pathetically weak response. Did this father have no backbone? Did he lack any concern whatsoever for his own honor? Why would he truckle to the demands of a rebellious son like this? Why not assert his authority as head of his own household and utterly disown the boy? By capitulating to his son's unreasonable request and simply handing over his own livelihood, the father would be as much an object of shame as the rebellious son. In fact, the Pharisees would no doubt regard the father as even *more* shameful than the son at this point because, in giving up his livelihood, he was in effect handing over the family honor and giving the boy license to trample it.

> The Prodigal took his portion of the family wealth without looking back. He had exactly what he wanted: absolute freedom.

The way the original text is worded is significant. "Livelihood" is a translation of *bios*, the Greek word for life. He divided up and gave his sons his whole life—his living, his livelihood, and everything the family had accumulated for generations. The fact that the younger boy was free to take his father's bequest and go off into a far country suggests that the father gave the sons the family estate with no strings attached. He apparently extracted no promises in return and took no measures to force the younger son to show respect to tradition. The Prodigal took his portion of the family wealth without looking back. He had exactly what he wanted: absolute freedom.

Devotion for His Son

The father's actions demonstrate that he was a truly loving father—not a tyrant—and he was willing to endure the pain of spurned affections and public humiliation rather than disown his son. He voluntarily suffered what is arguably the most painful personal agony of all: the grief of tender love rejected. The father's love for this boy was obviously profound. And the greater the love, the greater the pain when that love is rebuffed.

This is especially amazing when we remind ourselves that Jesus is giving an illustration of His own love for sinners. And because Jesus is God incarnate—the Lord Himself in human flesh—we need to understand that the reaction of the Prodigal's father depicts the love of Jehovah for rebellious humanity. Although He is absolutely sovereign and has both the power and the prerogative to destroy every sinner in an instant, He nevertheless extends to every person generous measures of mercy, loving-kindness, goodwill, and long-suffering. Like the father in the parable, rather than summarily disowning and destroying sinners as quickly as possible, God shows extreme forbearance. He gives them freedom to pursue their own self-will—even though it is clear that their only intention is rebellion against *His* will, and even though their rebellion seems for the moment to cause Him great dishonor.

> The reaction of the Prodigal's father depicts God's love for rebellious humanity.

But "dishonor" was nothing to Christ, who stepped out of heaven and away from His rightful throne as God. Instead, He "made Himself of no reputation, taking the form of a bondservant, and coming in the likeness of men. And being found in appearance as a man, He humbled Himself and became obedient to the point of death, even the death of the cross" (Philippians 2:7–8). "For the joy that was set before Him [He] endured the cross, despising the shame" (Hebrews 12:2).

Among the outstanding truths we are about to see portrayed so vividly in this parable are these two outstanding facts: the shame He bore was *our* shame; and the eternal joy that was set before Him is best exemplified in His profound delight over the redemption of repentant sinners.

❧ F O U R ❧

His Shameful Misconduct

The younger son gathered all together, journeyed to a far country, and there
wasted his possessions with prodigal living.

—Luke 15:13

THERE WERE TWO DISTINCT STAGES IN THE PRODIGAL'S rebellion, both of which would utterly cover him with disgrace in the minds of Jesus' audience. We've seen phase one in the reprehensible way he treated his own father.

Phase two is worse yet. It begins with the boy's departure from his family's household and follows his journey out into the world. This part of the story culminates in the absolute meltdown of the Prodigal's life. His own lusts prove uncontrollable. He finds himself enslaved in a horrific bondage from which he is powerless to free himself. It's the bondage of his own sin, and it turns out to be an infinitely worse kind of imprisonment for him than he ever imagined his father's authority to be. He is pulled progressively downward in sin's death spiral until he finds himself left virtually hopeless in the most appalling imaginable circumstances.

RUNNING AWAY

It didn't take long for the real agenda behind the Prodigal's defiance to become clear: "And *not many days after*, the younger son gathered

THE PRODIGAL SON

> Now that he
> finally had the
> means, he could
> hardly wait to
> make his escape.

all together, journeyed to a far country, and there wasted his possessions with prodigal living" (Luke 15:13; emphasis added). This young man was fed up with all his responsibilities, tired of being accountable to his father, and sick of every relationship in his life—especially with his father and older brother. Now that he finally had the means, he could hardly wait to make his escape.

Liquidating His Assets

The phrase "gathered all together" means that the Prodigal liquidated whatever he could, turning his inheritance into ready cash. The haste with which he acted suggests that he lost a tremendous amount of his legacy's value in the process.

Remember, as we have already seen, Moses' law had strict regulations governing the sale of real estate. Family lands were protected by these laws just so that no clan ever lost its property if one family member foolishly decided to squander his future this way. In Leviticus 25:23, the Lord says, "The land shall not be sold permanently, for the land is Mine."

As we noted in the previous chapter, land sales in Israel were therefore more like long-term leases. Family properties were redeemable, and land would always revert to the original owner's family in the year of Jubilee. (The Jubilee years occurred every half century, at the end of seven cycles of Sabbath years, per Leviticus 25:8–55.) The price on a plot of land was determined accordingly. The closer you were to the next Jubilee year, the less money you could get for land.

Furthermore, because of the tradition that prohibited a son from disposing of his father's property during the father's lifetime (as mentioned in the previous chapter), the only way to liquidate estate goods like this would be to sell most of the assets with the stipula- tion that the purchaser could not take possession until the death of the father. The Prodigal would virtually have to sell his birthright in garage-sale fashion on the futures market. Everything would be so heavily discounted that the vast majority of the value would be sacrificed in the process. He would be fortunate to get the equiva- lent of pennies on the dollar. In reality, he probably settled for much, much less. He just wanted out.

That perfectly illustrates the foolishness of the sinner. He wants to get away from God, and he is more concerned with doing it *now* than he is with what it might cost him in the future. He wants no accountability to God. He sells cheaply whatever good gifts he has received from God. He squanders spiritual opportunities, the benevolence of divine providence, and every blessing God ever bestows on him. He turns his nose up at the riches of God's good- ness, forbearance, and long-suffering, which *ought* to lead him to repentance (Romans 2:4).

Journeying to a Gentile Land

Remember, Jesus is telling this parable to Jewish leaders in a Jewish culture, so when he says the Prodigal "journeyed to a far country," they would instantly understand the implication. Any distant land would be a Gentile country. This young man left not only his home and family but also his cultural heritage and his faith.

> This young man left not only his home and family but also his cultural heritage and his faith.

This was yet another detail that evoked a sense of horror in Jesus' hearers. It was unthinkable that any Jewish young person would journey by choice into Gentile lands and willingly take up permanent residence there (or worse, become a vagrant so far from home) in order to indulge in licentious living. How bad was this kid? He was bad to the bone. He had so much scorn for his father that he deliberately exposed him to the most humiliating kind of public disgrace. That was bad enough. Add this boy's shallow materialism, his greed, his foolishness in forfeiting so much of the value of his heritage—and you already have a top-drawer delinquent. But when (on top of all that) the boy travels into a Gentile land to get as far away as he can from everyone who knew him—just so that he could indulge freely in evil behavior—he suddenly becomes such a hideously despicable figure that it would be hard to express his badness in mere words. How could there possibly be any more grotesque personification of evil and shame?

Surely Jesus was setting this guy up to be the main villain in the story. How could anyone be worse than this? Give him a funeral and invite the whole village. He's gone, and he's as good as dead. Right?

The scribes and Pharisees *must* have been thinking something like that at this point. Their contempt for wanton sinners was well known. That was after all the very thing that precipitated this exchange with Jesus in the first place. But even more than that, the thought of someone willingly forsaking home and religion, traveling into a far country, and taking up residence in a Gentile culture was unspeakably abhorrent to them. *Everything* in Gentile culture was unclean. No matter where he went and what he did after that, he would be hopelessly defiled in the Pharisees' estimation. The fact that he was doing this to wallow in sin on purpose was almost beyond comprehension. In their minds, the Prodigal was beyond redemption, and the father was well rid of him. No one could possibly be worse than someone who behaves like that.

Now hold that thought in your mind, and remember that the Prodigal Son's circumstances are actually going to get much worse before his case gets better.

WHERE IS THE ELDER BROTHER?

But where is the elder brother in all this? He is utterly absent from
the story at this point, and I'm convinced that is not without significance. Why doesn't he rise to the defense of the father's honor?
Why doesn't he step in and try to talk some sense into his younger
brother? Why do we hear neither a peep of protest nor a word of
gratitude from the elder brother when the father divides his livelihood and divests himself of everything he owns?

Surely the elder brother understood full well that his father was
bearing terrible public humiliation because of his younger brother's
rebellion. Why isn't there a verse telling us how he went out after
the younger brother and tried to bring him home? Why isn't there
anything here that might at least hint to us that he was personally
wounded over the grief of his father and the ruin of his brother?

Answer: because the elder brother didn't really have any
relationship with his father either. He had no more love for his
father than his prodigal brother did.
He was happy just to get his share
and stay home, basking in the community's impression that he was the
"good" son. His real character will
become clear shortly.

> The elder brother
> didn't really love
> his father any
> more than the
> Prodigal Son did.

But for now, take note: this
scene is filled with shame. This
was a totally dysfunctional family.
Although the father was a loving,
generous, kindly man who provided abundant gifts for his two
sons, both of his sons cared more for the father's wealth than they
did for the father himself. One was a flagrant, rebellious, and irre-
ligious sinner; the other was a religious sinner with a thin veneer
of respectability. Neither son had any authentic respect for the
father, and neither returned his love or showed any interest in a

right relationship with him. As a matter of fact, both sons hated the father, and they hated each other.

THE ROAD TO RUIN

The Prodigal seems to have made a beeline for the furthest point he could find away from home and responsibility. He "journeyed to a far country" (v. 13). Who knows how he chose which direction to travel or even if he had a particular place in mind for his final destination? If his thinking was typical of young people who follow this pattern of behavior, he probably headed off in the general direction of some place he'd heard about that sounded exotic.

But he had little knowledge of what real life would be like there. He had not considered what dangers might lurk there. And he clearly had given no forethought to the question of what would be involved in establishing a new life in a foreign culture. Evidently, getting established wasn't even part of his long-term plan. The Prodigal was simply looking for pleasure. And let's be honest: people who think like that typically don't think very far ahead.

> The Prodigal was simply looking for pleasure. And let's be honest: people who think like that typically don't think very far ahead.

So it's no huge surprise when we read in verse 13 that he "wasted his possessions with prodigal living." That's the direction the Prodigal's rebellion had been propelling him from the start. The Greek word translated "wasted" is *diaskorpizō*. It's a word that evokes the idea of winnowing, where you throw grain in the air and let the wind blow the chaff away. It literally means "to scatter abroad." He just flung it away—"with prodigal living." He squandered a fortune in no time, spending his inheritance in the pursuit of wickedness.

The elder brother later summed up the Prodigal's lifestyle in these words: he "devoured [his father's] livelihood with harlots" (v. 30). Some interpreters suggest that may be a mean-spirited exaggeration and thus a false accusation on the part of the older brother, designed to put the Prodigal in an even worse light than he deserved. But I'm inclined to think otherwise. If the Prodigal was completely innocent of that charge, I think Jesus would have said so, because it would have reinforced His case against the elder son's own bad attitude. But far from describing the Prodigal Son as someone who wasn't really as bad as people thought, Jesus was deliberately portraying him as someone so thoroughly debauched that he would be capable of practically anything. The clear implication of the expression "prodigal living" ("riotous living" in the KJV) is that he pursued a lifestyle of utter dissipation and gross immorality that was far-flung and uninhibited by any kind of scruple. His conscience was totally seared, or else he would not have pursued the course he did in the first place. And if he could spend away the family fortune so rapidly without spending any money on loose women, he probably spent it for something even worse.

Of course, anyone who spurns every duty, casts off all responsibility, flees every hint of accountability, and pursues that kind of immoral lifestyle is going to come to total ruin in no time at all. It's inevitable. It's a law built into the very fabric of creation and strictly enforced by the operations of divine providence. "Whatever a man sows, that he will also reap. For he who sows to his flesh will of the flesh reap corruption" (Galatians 6:7–8). That is precisely what happened to this fellow. He trashed his own life.

Sin never delivers what it promises, and the pleasurable life sinners think they are pursuing always turns out to be precisely the opposite: a hard road that inevitably leads to ruin and the ultimate, literal dead end. "The wages of sin is death" (Romans 6:23).

"If you live according to the flesh you will die" (Romans 8:13). "Sin, when it is full-grown, brings forth death" (James 1:15). The Prodigal was about to discover those truths in a very painful and vivid way.

> Sin never delivers what it promises, and the pleasurable life sinners think they are pursuing always turns out to be precisely the opposite: a hard road that inevitably leads to ruin and the ultimate, literal dead end.

His downfall was as sudden as it was inevitable: "But when he had spent all . . ." (Luke 15:14). The language suggests that when the Prodigal arrived in the far country, his fortune was still at least partially intact. He came as a fat cat, the new guy in town with a big bankroll. Here was a naive boy from far away with a big wad—and you can bet every con artist and lowlife in town set their sights on him.

The Prodigal was young and gullible and probably quite happy to be the center of attention at first. He had gone off in search of a fun-filled life, and now just look at him! Everyone in town who knew how to party wanted to be close to him. Cultivating that image was all he could think about. He wanted people to think he was generous, fun-loving, open-minded, and promiscuous. So he went on a wild spree. For a moment, he must have thought he had exactly what he wanted.

But whatever "friends" the Prodigal made in the pursuit of such a lifestyle were no true friends at all. They were just riffraff and scum who wanted to cash in on his foolish generosity. When he ran out of money, these "friends" would forsake him too.

That is exactly what happened. He "spent all" (v. 14). Squandered his fortune. Wasted his father's livelihood on worldly entertainments (v. 30). And most likely, the elder brother was exactly right: that included prostitutes and other similarly immoral activities.

Without meaning it in an overly harsh way, let's say the Prodigal got exactly what he deserved. He reaped what he sowed. He was left with absolutely nothing, and that was entirely his own fault.

> Without meaning it in an overly harsh way, let's say the Prodigal got exactly what he deserved. He reaped what he sowed.

PURSUED BY PROVIDENCE

Right after the money ran out, "there arose a severe famine in that land" (v. 14). The famine was not the Prodigal's fault, of course, but that's how life is. Some disasters we bring on ourselves, and sometimes calamity strikes through no particular fault of our own.

For someone like this rebellious youth, in a state of rebellion against both his God and his father, the conflux of so many severe setbacks at once must have felt like divinely orchestrated payback for his sin. In this case especially, we probably are supposed to detect an element of divine chastening in all that befell the Prodigal as his life unraveled. But because of his rebellion, he had nowhere to turn to find relief.

Here was an absolutely devastating turn of events. Consider how hard it must have hit the Prodigal. His whole life until now had been pillowed with comforts he simply took for granted. The prosperity and relative ease of his early home life had been bought and paid for by the hard work and frugal diligence of many generations of his ancestors. His father had met his every need and supplied him wth every amenity from the day he was born. He probably assumed (as many naive young people do) that life was naturally easy. He had no regard for the faithfulness of his fore-fathers who had all helped make his life so comfortable—and the proof of his shortsighted lack of appreciation is seen in the thoughtless way he so thoroughly abandoned his roots in quest of fleshly self-gratification.

Now the life of pleasure the Prodigal sought had not only come to a screeching halt but also it was suddenly clear to him that the life of freedom he thought he would find was nothing like he antici-pated. He had practically sold his soul for a gullible boy's daydream, and Providence was now demanding the immediate settlement of all accounts—with interest. The sudden string of setbacks was demoralizing in the extreme; it was emotionally draining, and it put him in a completely untenable situation economically. Jesus' description of the boy's dilemma is a major understatement: "he began to be in want" (v. 14). A major famine at this moment was just about the worst thing that could possibly happen to him—at least from an earthly perspective.

> A major famine at this moment was just about the worst thing that could possibly happen to him—at least from an earthly perspective.

What, precisely, would be involved when poverty and destitution are intensified by famine? Famines are almost unheard of in our culture, so we might read that verse without experiencing quite the same sense of horror Jesus' original audience would have felt as the tale unfolded. We need to pause here and reflect on the implications of verse 14.

Famines were common enough in Jesus' time that He did not have to explain the Prodigal Son's dilemma to His audience. It would be seen—especially by the scribes and Pharisees—as a stroke of divine chastisement.

Numerous famines of various sizes and duration occurred during the long period of history covered by Scripture. The first one we read about is in Genesis 12:10. That famine drove Abraham to Egypt, and it appears to be the first in a cycle of similar waves of extreme hunger that struck the Promised Land. Thus a famine in Isaac's era drove him to Egypt as well (Genesis 26:10). And the famous seven-year famine that Joseph foresaw in a dream (Genesis 41:54) was the occasion for Jacob's entire family to seek refuge in Egypt. That's the whole reason the original Israelites, at the start of the book of Exodus, were living in Egypt as slaves of Pharaoh and in need of a deliverer like Moses.

Famines were therefore seen as uniquely providential disasters— in most cases clear tokens of the most severe degree of divine displeasure. In fact, since famines were usually caused by other disasters, they often seemed like an exclamation mark at the end of a series of compounded misfortunes. (That is one factor that made this famine in the case of the Prodigal Son seem so poignant and so fitting.)

A famine could be caused, for example, by drought (1 Kings 17:1), by insects (Joel 1:14), by hailstorms (Exodus 9:22–23), by enemies who laid seige to cities (2 Kings 6:25), and even by the destructive behaviors of marauding, nomadic peoples like the Amalekites, who traveled in massive armies and devoured everything in their path (Deuteronomy 28:21). Scripture describes one famine so severe in Samaria during the lifetime of Elisha that two women made a pact to cook and eat their own babies. The women actually ate one of the babies, but since the mother of the other child was no longer so desperately hungry, she refused to give up her own child to be eaten (2 Kings 6:26–31).

That kind of desperate hunger is hard to imagine for those of us who live in places that have fast-food restaurants at every major intersection. But in most of sub-Saharan Africa, including several populous countries (especially Somalia, Sudan, Ethiopia, and Chad), famine is a regular threat to life. Those parts of the world have all experienced terrible waves of devastating famine in our generation. So the awful reality of this kind of disaster still plagues large parts of the world's population today, and it is to our shame that so many who live in industrialized cultures are not more aware than they are of the human cost of this type of disaster.

A severe famine is one of the worst disasters that can befall a nation. Here's author William Manchester's short description of famines in Europe during the medieval era:

> The years of hunger were terrible. The peasants might be forced to sell all they owned. . . . In the hardest times they devoured bark, roots, grass; even white clay. Cannibalism was not unknown. Strangers and travelers were waylaid and killed to be eaten, and there are tales of gallows being torn down—as many as twenty bodies would hang from a single scaffold—by men frantic to eat the warm flesh raw.[1]

I have read numerous firsthand descriptions of famine even in more recent centuries. There was the potato famine (sometimes called the Great Hunger) in mid-nineteenth-century Ireland. A million people—more than 10 percent of Ireland's population at the time—died of starvation over a three-year period. Even more recently was the Great Famine (the Holodomor) in Ukraine in the 1930s, in which multiple millions died of hunger. That famine is believed to have been deliberately caused by Stalin as an act of genocide.

Eyewitness accounts of these and other severe famines are difficult to read. But almost all of them have several features in common. They describe how people are driven mad by hunger. Acts of cannibalism are common. Death from hunger is often so widespread and frequent that bodies must be collected and removed each day. One writer tells of children being sold into slavery as an act of mercy, just to keep them from starving. Another writer tells of how the flesh of starvation victims is ground and sold as food. People resort to eating things such as grass, shoe leather, rotten flesh, garbage, and excrement. Entire towns and villages are left without inhabitants. It is an agonizing, unspeakably horrific, slow, hopeless disaster, filled with anguish and torment.

Unlike us, Jesus' listeners were not so far removed from famines that He needed to elaborate. The mention of "severe famine" would instantly conjure up a ghastly picture in their minds. They understood that He was describing a level of desperation far beyond anything most of us today can conceive of.

THE PARTY WAS OVER

This young man's life had become a nightmarish horror. He had made numerous bad decisions for himself, but now the hand of divine providence had made his troubles more severe than he could have imagined. This was life at its very lowest.

The scribes and Pharisees listening to the story were no doubt recoiling at the atrocity this young man's life had become. He had left a fine home and bright future under a wonderfully loving and generous father, and now he had come to this—without friends, family, or hope in a foreign land with nowhere to turn. The party was over for sure.

FIVE

His Turning Point

When he came to himself . . .

—Luke 15:17

THE PRODIGAL CERTAINLY DID NOT FIND THE KIND of life he wanted when he began his escapade. All the glitter was off the gold in the far country. The road he had chosen to follow turned out to be an expressway to destruction. His freewheeling lifestyle had suddenly morphed into a terrible, crushing bondage. All his dreams had become nightmares. All his pleasure had turned to pain. All his fun had given way to profound sorrow. And this heedless young rebel who threw everything away for a few moments of self-indulgence was now forced into a lifestyle of utter self-deprivation. The revelry had ended. The laughs had been silenced. The music had stopped playing. His so-called friends were all gone. It was as bad as it could get, and he was about to die.

> The road the Prodigal Son had chosen to follow turned out to be an expressway to destruction.

One thing is certain: if the Prodigal had known it would come to this, he never would have set out on his quest. He wanted unrestrained pleasure. He wanted his lusts fulfilled without interruption and without rebuke. What he got instead was unmitigated pain, loneliness, and the threat of imminent death. His life was now missing all the pleasures he ever dreamed about—and filled to overflowing with evils he had foolishly never envisioned.

The tenacity of some sinners is impossible to explain rationally. Some people are so determined to have their own way that even when they are being force-fed the distasteful consequences of their transgressions, they still will not give up the pursuit. I have known people whose lives were totally laid waste by the fallout of some favorite sin. They might literally be sick to death of their sin's repercussions, and yet they will not give up the sin itself. Sin is a bondage they are powerless to break.

That was (at first) the case with the Prodigal Son. Destitute, hopeless, and with his life lying in ruins all around him, he *still* was not quite ready to go home. Going home, of course, would mean confessing that he had been wrong and foolish. It also meant facing the resentment of his brother, owning up to the grief and heartache he had caused his father, and inviting public shame on his own head. Above all, it would mean accepting responsibility, living under accountability, and submitting to authority—all of which he had fled in the first place.

THE SCHEME TO AVOID REPENTANCE

The disillusioned Prodigal at first did what a lot of people try to do before they truly hit bottom. He desperately attempted to concoct a scheme that would enable him to weather the crisis and perhaps avoid truly having to face his sin and own up fully to all the wrong he had done.

His only thought all along, of course, had been to get out from under his father's authority so he could spend the rest of his life doing whatever he wanted. That plan (such as it was) really didn't work out for him at all. So here was his plan B: "He went and joined himself to a citizen of that country, and he sent him into his fields to feed swine" (Luke 15:15).

Apparently, the first thing the Prodigal said to himself when his world fell apart was, *I need to find a job*. He thought he could pick himself up—maybe even work his way out of the dilemma. That is typical of sinners on the run from God. They live a dissolute, rebellious life and indulge in sin to their heart's content, only to end up bankrupt, depleted of all their strength—and ultimately on skid row, figuratively if not literally. Yet they often reassure themselves with the notion that they have the means and the ability to work their way out of the mess they have made of their lives.

> He thought he could pick himself up—maybe even work his way out of the dilemma. That is typical of sinners on the run from God.

Some people waste years under that delusion, and for many it becomes a pathway to destruction they never escape from.

Joining Himself to a Citizen

What does it mean that the Prodigal "joined himself to a citizen of that country"? A "citizen" in the days of Rome spoke of a privileged person. Someone could even be a native of a certain region and still not be a citizen. In fact, in lands controlled by Rome, citizens were usually very wealthy foreigners. That's because the word spoke of *Roman* citizenship. With it came a vast amount of privilege and honor.

The Prodigal Son had somehow become acquainted with at least one of these persons of means—probably an individual with whom he had once participated in some vice or amusement. Scripture says he "joined himself" to the citizen. The Greek text employs a very picturesque verb—*kollaô*, which literally means to "glue". The implication is that this relationship wasn't the citizen's idea. The Prodigal affixed himself to this one influential person whom he somehow knew from his days of extravagance, and he refused to go away. He stuck to him like epoxy.

In other words, the Prodigal's desperation had already reached such a critical point that he literally became a beggar. By now he was probably filthy, unkempt, reduced to extreme poverty, and all he could do was beg.

Even today, this kind of scene is fairly common in undeveloped countries. Having traveled occasionally in some of the poorest parts of the world, I have experienced this many times. Some beggars simply will not let you walk away, even if you give them alms. They will hang on to your coat, pull on your arm, grab at your pockets, and overwhelm you with sheer desperation. The imagery Jesus' story conjures up is of that kind of beggar, and it suggests that the citizen was not instantly responsive to the Prodigal's pleas. But the desperate boy stuck to him as if he had been hot-glued, pleading over and over for help.

The Prodigal Son's behavior at this point is reminiscent of the widow in the parable of Luke 18:1–8, who attached herself to an unjust judge and persistently, relentlessly demanded justice. The reluctant judge finally granted her wish even though it was contrary to his own preferences, saying, "Though I do not fear God nor regard man, yet because this widow troubles me I will avenge her, lest by her continual coming she weary me" (Luke 18:4–5).

A similar dynamic was at work here. Nothing in the text suggests that this citizen had an ounce of genuine compassion for the Prodigal. In fact, the evidence points to the opposite conclusion. And yet the Prodigal finally gained a hearing and was given a job: feeding pigs.

Feeding the Pigs

This was no real employment at all. Swineherding paid next to nothing—not enough even to meet the immediate needs of the Prodigal. Feeding pigs was also extremely demeaning work. It was virtually the lowest possible chore in the whole hierarchy of labor. It required no skill whatsoever, so this was a role often given to people who were mentally deficient, bereft of all social skills, or otherwise unfit for life in polite society. Remember that the demon-possessed man in Gadara was living in a place where swine fed (Mark 5:11).

Even today, with modern technology and streamlined farming methods, pig farming is among the most despicable, noxious, and foul-smelling livestock business. Processed pig feed is available nowadays, but it is expensive. (It's also sickeningly fetid even in the best cases. There's no way to make pig farming an aesthetically appealing enterprise.) So it's quite common for hog farmers simply to collect spoiled food garbage and feed the pigs with mounds of rubbish. Pigs, of course, are quite happy to eat virtually anything that's even remotely digestible.

One of the cable television networks that specializes in educational documentaries recently did a feature about a large hog farm in Nevada, focusing on the means by which they feed their animals. They start by collecting massive amounts of garbage from the Las Vegas strip, where several tons of spoiled or leftover food are thrown away daily from the casinos' extravagant buffets. Those leftovers are systematically gathered and hauled to the pig farm in enormous slop trucks.

In the desert heat, by the time the garbage arrives at the farm, it has already blended into a tank of nauseating semiliquid stew. The stench from so much decomposing food must likewise be virtually unbearable. The slop is poured onto a kind of flumelike conveyor system where workers take out as many pieces as possible of various plastic food containers and other nonbiodegradables. The stream of spoiled food is channeled into a two-story-tall kettle, where the whole mess is cooked in order to eliminate the worst bacteria. The resulting goulash is then allowed to cool. By then it's a nondescript, chunky, gloppy, bile-colored goo.

That substance is poured by bucketfuls into long, filthy troughs that are permanently caked with large amounts of mud and pig excrement. Even as workers fill the troughs, however, the pigs squeal with delight and push one another aside, positioning themselves under the streams of pig slop while it is being poured from the buckets. The swine eagerly devour gallons of the stuff within moments. Sickening as it was to watch (or even read about), the news program graphically demonstrated that pigs will eat anything.

> The nature of the job alone was automatically enough to seal the Prodigal Son's status as a permanent, irredeemable outcast in Israel.

For the Prodigal Son, born under the law of Moses, pigs were considered ceremonially unclean animals. That meant any kind of contact with the animals was considered spiritually defiling. Moreover, since it was forbidden to eat pork as food, to participate in raising hogs for human consumption was considered grossly immoral—especially in the eyes of scribes and Pharisees. So the nature of the job alone was automatically enough to seal the Prodigal Son's status as a permanent, irredeemable outcast in Israel.

This also suggests the job offer was really more of an insult than an act of compassion. The wealthy citizen seems to have proposed the job because it was the best way to unglue himself from this tenaciously determined beggar. Accepting the job required the Prodigal to stay where the pigs were—which was surely a far enough distance away from their wealthy owner that he wasn't constantly subjected to their noise and aroma. Although the English text describes the pigs' dwelling place as "fields," it actually would have been a remote, harsh, rocky wilderness where nothing could grow besides tangled scrub. Don't imagine that the pigs occupied any kind of lush agricultural field or grassland. Famine or not, hogs being raised for market were always consigned to wilderness land that was useless for any other purpose because pigs are destructive to valuable crops and gardens.

With absolutely no other options, the Prodigal accepted the job and went to work. The citizen "sent him into his fields to feed swine" (v. 15). That means the Prodigal took up permanent residence out in the harsh wilderness, living with the hogs. He became a full-time swineherd.

Here was another intensely revolting turn of the plot as far as the scribes and Pharisees were concerned. They no doubt gasped yet again at the thought of this Jewish boy, who not only accepted employment on a hog farm but also went to live among the swine. The imagery Jesus constructed was already excruciatingly abhorrent in their eyes, and yet with every new detail He added, the picture became bleaker. Could it get any worse?

Yes, it could. And it did.

THE LOW POINT OF THIS DISASTER

Obviously, in a time of severe famine, even pigs' food would be meager. These particular pigs were fortunate enough to have a shrewd and wealthy owner who continued feeding and fattening them—rather than immediately selling them for slaughter. He was probably saving them while the famine grew worse. He would sell them later at premium prices. Meanwhile, the pigs could be fed with stuff like husks, rinds, eggshells, and various leafy stalks or cane plants. Those things are all indigestible by humans. In fact, they are edible only with great difficulty even for pigs. In all likelihood, these were by no means well-fed pigs. It was, after all, a time of severe famine.

Longing to Eat Pig Slop

But at least the pigs still had *some* kind of food. The Prodigal was literally starving to death even while he watched the hungry pigs eat. Contemplating that fact, he found himself burning with jealousy toward the pigs! Jesus said, "He would gladly have filled his stomach with the pods that the swine ate" (v. 16).

The Greek word translated "pods" is *keration*—a word signifying carob pods. These were long string-bean-shaped seed pods that grew on scrubby, treelike bushes. The beans inside the pods were hard, and the pod shells were tough and leathery. A powder made from the ground beans is sometimes used as a substitute for chocolate. A kind of molasses can also be extracted from the beans, and that was an important source of sugar in the ancient Middle East. Other than that, however, carob pods are inedible for humans and frankly not all that nutritious even for livestock. But the trees are amazingly hardy, so even during an intense drought or plague of insects, carob pods may yet be abundant. They have often been used as a supplement for livestock feed in times of famine, and animals such as pigs and cattle can subsist on a steady diet of carob pods when necessary. That's exactly what was happening here.

As the Prodigal watched the swine greedily devouring those carob pods, he found himself earnestly longing to fill his own stomach with the swine food. If only those pods were edible for him! "He would *gladly* have filled his stomach" with them (v. 16; emphasis added).

Treated as One of the Pigs

That was yet another detail in Jesus' story that surely caused the scribes and Pharisees to recoil in disgust. If they were provoked and outraged by the fact that Jesus sat at the same table with tax collectors and other sinners, how much more revolting was the thought of a youth from a good Jewish home descending so low into sin that he found himself longing to share food with pigs! In the Pharisees' estimation, he had essentially *become* one of the pigs. The only way he could get any lower was to be cast into the pit of hell—which, as far as the Pharisees were concerned, was practically unavoidable for him now and a punishment well deserved.

Even in that distant Gentile land where practically no one was constrained by any scruples about ceremonial uncleanness or terribly repulsed by the eating of pork, the Prodigal's station in life was now such that he was deemed untouchable. "No one gave him anything" (v. 16).

> The only way he could get any lower was to be cast into the pit of hell—which, as far as the Pharisees were concerned, was practically unavoidable for him now.

The typical reader today cannot even begin to understand how loathsome the Prodigal would seem to the highbrow scribes and Pharisees—obsessed as they were with abstaining from all kinds of ceremonial pollution. As Jesus told this parable, he had ascribed to the Prodigal every kind of defilement, disgrace, and dishonor imaginable. Every detail Jesus mentioned about him further offended the sensitivities of the religious elite. Because of all the various ways this young rebel had defiled and disgraced himself, by the time Jesus got to this point in the tale, the Prodigal Son was (by the Pharisees' way of thinking) quite clearly an object worthy of more contempt than pity. He was so utterly covered with reproach and ill repute that they had no doubt completely written him off as irredeemable.

THE GREAT LESSON OF THE PRODIGAL'S RUIN

Before we move on, a vital lesson about the nature of sin and its destruction needs to be drawn from the wreckage of the Prodigal Son's life. His experience is a vivid picture of what sin is and what it does to people. The Prodigal Son is a living symbol of every sinner who has ever lived—including you and me. And therefore we need to pay careful attention to the warning Jesus gives us in this part of the parable.

> The Prodigal Son is a living symbol of every sinner who has ever lived—including you and me.

All sin involves precisely this kind of irrational rebellion against a loving heavenly Father. Sin's greatest evil lies not in the fact that it is a transgression of the Law—although it most certainly is that (1 John 3:4). But the real wickedness of sin stems from its nature as a personal affront to a good and gracious Lawgiver. Our sin is a calculated, deliberate violation of the relationship we have with our Creator. (You may never have consciously considered sin that way before, but it is nevertheless true, and every person's conscience affirms that reality. The secrets of our heart bear witness against us, and Romans 2:14–16 says even those secrets will one day be made manifest and judged by God.)

When we sin, we show disdain for God's fatherly love as well as His holy authority. We spurn not merely His law, but also His very person. To sin is to deny God His place. It is an expression of hatred against God. It is tantamount to wishing He were dead. It is dishonoring to Him. And since all sin has at its heart this element of contempt for God, even the smallest sin has enough evil to unleash an eternity full of mischief, misfortune, and misery. The fact that the entire world of human evil all stemmed from Adam's simple act of disobedience is vivid proof of that (Romans 5:12, 19; 1 Corinthians 15:21–22).

Moreover, sin *always* bears evil fruit. We cannot take the good gifts God has surrounded us with, barter them away as if they were nothing, and then not expect to reap the consequences of spiritual poverty that are the inevitable result.

Here's a shocking reality: the Prodigal Son is not merely a picture of the worst of sinners; he is a symbol of *every* unredeemed sinner—alienated from God and without a hope in the world (Ephesians 2:12). He is a precise and living effigy of the entire human race—fallen, sinful, and rebellious. Worse yet, his character reflects not only the state

> To sin is to deny God His place. It is an expression of hatred against God. It is tantamount to wishing He were dead.

of our fallen race as a whole but also the natural condition of every individual ever conceived by a human father since the fall of Adam. We all begin this life with our backs turned against God; desiring to flee far from Him, with no regard for His love, no appreciation of His generosity, and no respect for His honor.

It's true: the evil motives that drove the Prodigal are the natural tendencies of every fallen human heart. "The carnal mind is enmity against God; for it is not subject to the law of God, nor indeed can be. So then, those who are in the flesh cannot please God" (Romans 8:7–8). We are "by nature children of wrath," born with a sinful nature and helplessly dominated by fleshly desires (Ephesians 2:2–3).

> We are *all* prodigal sons and daughters.

In other words, we are *all* prodigal sons and daughters. Every one of us is guilty of self-indulgence, dissipation, and unrestrained lust. We have been heedless to the consequences of sin and reckless in the pursuit of evil. Apart from God's restraining grace, every one of us would have long ago sold our birthright, wasted our lives, and squandered every blessing God has given us—trading away His bountiful, daily goodness in exchange for a brief moment of cheap self-gratification.

Perhaps you feel you *have* done those things. Welcome to the world of prodigal sons and daughters.

The end of this young man's journey in the pig field perfectly exemplifies the destruction and heartache to which sin inevitably leads. It is the very image of spiritual bankruptcy, emptiness, destitution, and loneliness. At the end of that broad road is nothing but destruction. There is no one there to help, nowhere to turn, and no earthly hope left.

Here the foolish sinner has exhausted his best plan B and must realize that it never could have worked in the first place. We lack the ability to repair our own broken lives. We can't possibly atone for the sins we have committed, so we can't make our guilt go away. There is absolutely no earthly answer for such a dilemma. It will not be found in psychology, group therapy, or self-help—and it is certainly not found in drugs, alcohol, or any other form of escape. You can't get away from sin's consequences by moving to a new neighborhood, by marrying a new partner, or by otherwise running away. When all such attempts at evading sin's payday are finally exhausted, the sinner truly hits rock bottom.

Unless a gracious Savior can be found, nothing awaits but death and eternal doom.

THE WAKE-UP CALL

That's precisely where the Prodigal Son finally found himself. He was one of those fortunate sinners who "came to himself" (v. 17) before reaping the full and final wages of sin. The phrase actually means that he came to the *end* of himself—or in the words of a different translation, "he came to his senses" (NASB).

Working in the fields with the pigs turned out providentially to the Prodigal's eternal benefit. This young man who had been so intoxicated with worldly fun, earthly pleasures, and the companionship of evil people was finally forced to a place of solitude—perhaps for the first time in his short, irresponsible life. There he had to face soberly and earnestly the ugly reality of what he had become. As he watched the pigs eat those tough, tasteless pods (nothing more than indigestible garbage to him), he caught himself longing to fill his stomach with *that*.

No wonder he came to his senses. Watching those filthy hogs wallowing in the squalid mire and pushing one another aside while hungrily devouring refuse, he might well have been watching his own life in the mirror. No sinner was ever brought face-to-face with a more vivid image of the life of sin (cf. 2 Peter 2:22).

Here the plot finally turns in a direction that is a great relief to those of us who have actually lived the Prodigal's story. We can identify with his plight. We have tasted the bitterness of sin's guilt and felt the hopelessness of its bondage. And we are eager for the Prodigal Son to find deliverance.

Here comes the part of the parable we have been waiting for. It is the central turning point in the parable of the prodigal son: "He came to himself" (Luke 15:17).

I like that expression, because it tacitly acknowledges what the sober listener will have suspected all along: up to this point, the Prodigal Son was *beside himself*—out of his mind. That's

Here comes the part of the parable we have been waiting for. . . . "He came to himself" (Luke 15:17).

not to suggest that he was actually suffering from some kind of clinical dementia or mental illness. But he was pursuing a way of life that was nothing less than moral insanity. Every chapter of human history and the personal experiences of multitudes all testify that the lifestyle the Prodigal chose is a fast track to homelessness, misery, and utter despair—and it *does* sometimes drive people to literal insanity.

Beside Himself Spiritually

Indeed, the course of this young man's decline perfectly illustrates why sin itself is just spiritual madness. Think back through his journey so far. From the time he demanded his inheritance until the moment he finally hit bottom in the pig wallow, nothing he did made any rational sense. He had no plan or purpose. He never counted the cost. He just wanted to indulge in selfish pleasures without any boundaries or restrictions. So he set off on a directionless quest for unbridled "freedom" and lavish living.

But instead of luxury and liberty, he found precisely the opposite. He not only squandered his rich legacy, but he was also caught in the profoundest state of bondage. Everything he had sought, he lost. Yet right up until this very moment, he had continued in the path of sin. He was certainly beside himself spiritually.

Beside Himself Mentally

And the further he pursued that course, the more he acted as if he were mentally unhinged too. Having squandered a fortune on sinful pleasures, the Prodigal found himself desiring to fill up with inedible pig slop. His desperate, irrational thoughts and behaviors were certainly characteristic of a complete lunatic.

As a matter of fact, to any objective observer who might have encountered him in the fields living with pigs, the Prodigal probably seemed very much like a madman. Such is the cruelty of sin's bondage.

Sin, of course, is inherently irrational. We might well describe sin itself as a kind of moral madness. Sin is the creature's rebellion against the Creator, and that doesn't make sense on any scale. But the absurdity of sin is often particularly obvious in cases of gross sin, prolonged sin, and certain kinds of deliberate sin. As a pastor, I frequently see people who have foolishly forfeited life's best blessings—sacificing family, job, and reputation—in a mad quest for the pleasures of sin (which are only fleeting and illusory anyway).

Instead of the pleasure they hoped for, they become chronically depressed, angry, antisocial, and more and more irrational. In that way, sin can indeed drive someone to literal insanity.

Most big-city rescue missions are full of people who once functioned on a fairly normal level as productive members of society but who were driven to homelessness, despair, and the brink of madness because they mindlessly pursued some favorite sin without considering the potential consequences.

The Prodigal Son was well on the road to that kind of insanity.

> His first instinct upon regaining his senses was to plan how he might get back to his father and his home.

Coming to Himself

At last, however, just when all hope for the younger brother would seem to be extinguished, "he came to himself." He woke up to reality. In the solitude of the pig fields, he was forced to face what he had become, and that somehow jolted him out of utter insensibility. Suddenly, he began to think clearly. His first instinct upon regaining his senses was to plan how he might get back to his father and his home. With all his resources spent and all his companions gone, he had nowhere else to go and no other means by which to survive. He was truly at the end of the road.

So for the first time in his life, the younger son was determined to walk away from his sin, plead for his father's forgiveness, and submit to his father's authority. He turned and headed home.

SIX

His Return

And he arose and came to his father . . .

—Luke 15:20

FOR THE SCRIBES AND PHARISEES, THE NOTION THAT someone like the Prodigal Son could ever find any kind of forgiveness or redemption was far beyond their comprehension. In the first place, they would automatically take a cynical view of every token of repentance coming from someone who had sunk as low as this.

Second, their whole concept of righteousness was faulty, because it was based largely on a legal merit system. The scribes and Pharisees thought people could *become* righteous through lifelong devotion to a complex system of religious works. They followed an exacting process of ceremonial obedience to Moses' law, with particular emphasis on cosmetic details and picayune trivialities. Worse yet, they had overlaid the law of God with a perplexing labyrinth of useless human traditions. All of that needed to be observed diligently over a lifetime, they believed, for anyone to be deemed righteous. So they had no category in their theological system to account for how someone like the Prodigal Son could ever be saved from the wrath of God and brought into divine favor.

A Surprising Twist in the Story

Luke describes the Pharisees as those who "trusted in themselves that they were righteous, *and despised others*" (Luke 18:9; emphasis added). In their view, hatred for a rebel like this was justified. They assumed the Prodigal was beyond saving, and in fact, they were perfectly happy for him to receive the just deserts of his sin. As far as they were concerned, the Prodigal's repentance was an unwelcome kink in a story that already had a very clear-cut lesson about the due consequences of sin. They were prepared to affirm that lesson— until the Prodigal repented. Then suddenly, the central figure in Jesus' tale became a serious challenge to their religious system.

But in Jesus' telling of the parable, the Prodigal Son's crisis in the pig fields was a turning point, not the end of the story. The Prodigal *did* repent. And it was not merely a superficial ploy to regain his father's sympathy, or a quick-and-dirty scheme to recover the comforts of his old life.

This was heartfelt, deep repentance, and we see its genuineness in every step of the plan the Prodigal carefully outlined for his return to the father's household. Every aspect of his repentance was thought through. He finally realized how egregiously he had sinned against his father. He could now see that his father had *always* been gracious and good. And he finally acknowledged that he himself had been wrong—it was entirely his own fault (and his own sin) that brought him so low. He confessed freely that he was not worthy of any more grace or favor.

And yet the Prodigal planned to appeal to the father's great loving-kindness anyway: "When he came to himself, he said, 'How many of my father's hired servants have bread enough and to spare, and I perish with hunger! I will arise and go to my father, and will say to him, Father, I have sinned against heaven and before you, and I am no longer worthy to be called your son. Make me like one of your hired servants'" (Luke 15:17–19).

That was the *new* plan, and it was a good one. Rather than trying to evade responsibility for his sin, the younger son would face it squarely. Rather than running further away, he would go home. He would make a full confession and throw himself on his father's mercy. This was, after all, his one remaining hope.

The love of self and sin that had once made him so blind was now gone. He was finally seeing things clearly. In the wake of all the disaster his sin had brought crashing down around him, everything he once spurned and left behind began to look appealing. He knew he had permanently forfeited his rightful status as a son, but even being his father's hired servant would certainly beat feeding pigs for a living. Furthermore, whatever disgrace he might face by going back home was nothing compared to the shame of living with swine.

> He would make a full confession and throw himself on his father's mercy. This was, after all, his one remaining hope.

The brief insight Jesus gives into the heart and mind of the Prodigal is one of the best and clearest examples of true repentance in all of Scripture.

FACING REALITY

The first significant step in the Prodigal's return involved taking an honest look at his situation. That meant facing the ugly reality of what he had become, accepting responsibility for what he had done, owning up to the severity of his guilt, admitting his utter helplessness, and turning to someone who could truly help.

Here the father comes back into the story, and it is significant that the father's first point of reentry into the parable occurs in the mind of the Prodigal Son. The young man finally remembers his father. This is our first clue that a significant change has taken place in his heart—because this time when he thinks of his father, he doesn't shun the thought. In fact, he finds a ray of hope in the memory of his father's gracious loving-kindness. He said, "How many of my father's hired servants have bread enough and to spare?" (v. 17). Even the lowest of his father's hired servants fared better than he was doing out there on his own. He knew he did not deserve even a hired servant's status in his father's household, but he also knew his father to be generous, and that got him thinking.

How different this was from the boy's original, heedless, ungrateful attitude toward his father! It has seemed from the very start that his only motive with regard to the father was to get as far away as possible. Even running out of resources didn't immediately change his attitude. Remember, when this fool and his money were first parted, his initial response was to hire himself out to a citizen—whose character he seems to have badly misjudged. There was no suggestion at that point that he was thinking about his father at all.

In fact, if the Prodigal had given any thought to home and family at that juncture, he seems to have quickly put them out of his mind. Perhaps he wanted to avoid the humbling experience of admitting his wrong. He also knew in his heart that his father had every legitimate reason to treat him with severity rather than mercy. Evidently, he still held on to the delusion that by evading responsibility, accountability, and morality he could eventually gain the kind of liberty he sought.

But now finding himself alone and helplessly ensnared in a truly deadly kind of bondage, he finally realized the folly of that way of thinking. Sin might *promise* freedom from responsibility and moral constraints, but in reality, it always results in a much worse kind of slavery: the forced death-march of sin (Romans 6:16). Sinners caught in sin's web are helpless to extricate themselves or avoid the inevitable destruction sin causes. That's why the Prodigal's plan B—his best strategy for working his own way out of the mess he was in—was doomed from the start. The citizen from whom he sought help had essentially abandoned him to die in the fields with the pigs. Sin's companionships are always fickle like that.

But when the Prodigal was forced into virtual solitude, with all the time in the world to reflect, his thoughts finally turned to his father. And what stood out in the boy's mind was his father's kindness and generosity. His father also had hired servants—*many* of them. And every one of them had "bread enough and to spare" (v. 17).

> Sin might *promise* freedom from responsibility and moral constraints, but in reality, it always results in a much worse kind of slavery.

The younger son's next words are important because they succinctly and accurately express just how desperate his situation really was: "I perish with hunger!" (v. 17). The stark honesty of that admission is refreshing. It was no hyperbole. He literally was starving to death. He *would* die soon if he remained in these circumstances. The pangs of his hunger and the frightfulness of his situation obviously had him in an uncomfortable corner where that was practically all he could think about. But it's nevertheless significant that this is the first time he has spoken of what he truly and honestly *needed*, as opposed to what he merely *desired*.

Here, I am convinced, is where true repentance always begins: with an accurate assessment of one's own condition. Everyone—from the profligate sinner who is a complete wastrel (such as this young man) to the most fastidious, patronizing Pharisee—needs to face the reality that the sinfulness we have inherited from Adam has made us spiritual paupers. No sinner has the means to atone for his or her own sin or the ability to overcome the power of sin that holds us. Our sin has put us in a desperate situation.

Of course, that is much harder for a pompous, respectable sinner to acknowledge than it is for a wretched swineherd. "Those who are well have no need of a physician, but those who are sick" (Matthew 9:12). Multitudes are kept in spiritual darkness and under the condemnation of heaven because they simply refuse to confess how needy they are. That was precisely the situation the Pharisees were in.

> Here, I am convinced, is where true repentance always begins: with an accurate assessment of one's own condition.

The Prodigal, on the other hand, had already lost whatever pretense of dignity and self-confidence he once might have maintained. He no longer had any resources of his own, no one else gave him anything, and he couldn't even scavenge sufficient nourishment from the pigs' food. It was absolutely the end of the road for him, and he confessed that.

Simply and honestly facing the reality of his own circumstances is what caused such a monumental change in the Prodigal's attitude toward his father. Prior to this, he had not showed a hint of respect, affection, or even simple appreciation for his father. Now he was forced to confess that he would be vastly better off at the lowest level of servitude under his own father than far away in the pig fields, reaping the bitter fruits of his "freedom" and literally facing death as a reward for his foolish pursuit of selfish pleasure. He had stupidly spurned his father's jurisdiction when he held the status of a son. He was now perfectly willing to come back under his father's authority as a lowly hired servant. That would by any measure be a major step up from where he was now. Besides, it was the only way out of this mess that was open to him.

HIS ONLY HOPE:
PERMITTED TO BE A HIRED SERVANT

It was a truly amazing turnaround for the Prodigal Son to reach the point where he would even consider being a hired servant to his father, and it's a very clear indicator that he now realized just how low he had sunk. The Greek word translated "hired servants" in this verse is *misthios*. It refers to day laborers—the lowest of all workers on the economic scale. In the first-century culture, that kind of hired servant held a much lower status than a slave. Slaves were supplied with living quarters, clothing, and all the necessities of life. Trusted bondservants might even be put in charge of important business affairs, and they were rewarded when they served well (Matthew 25:14–25). Many household servants (especially in large estates) were educated, cultured, honorable, highly skilled people, whose status was anything but lowly. Nehemiah, serving as cupbearer to the king of Persia (Nehemiah 1:11), is one biblical example of a slave who enjoyed honor and advantage.

You can also see evidence of the relative comfort some slaves enjoyed in the ruins of ancient Pompeii, a resort town consisting largely of homes that belonged to wealthy Roman citizens. The entire town was preserved in near pristine condition under the ashes resulting from a catastrophic eruption of Vesuvius in AD 79. So in Pompeii we have a vivid snapshot of what life was like in the first century. I've had the privilege of walking through the city and some of the homes there on a couple of occasions. The typical household servant's living conditions were usually the most spartan rooms in the estates, of course. But all the servants' needs were supplied, and they lived in relative comfort. In some cases, they even enjoyed many luxuries.

Day laborers, on the other hand, were society's most desperately poor. Unlike slaves, they had no master continually caring for them. They were on their own, and they lived as best they could on whatever they could earn from day to day. Many of them were homeless and unskilled. They would therefore be given the most menial or undesirable work. They were usually hired to do temporary manual labor (during harvest season, for instance; cf. Matthew 20:1–16).

And they were paid a very meager wage. Usually the rate was determined at the start of the workday, but not always (vv. 13–15). A denarius for a full day's work was standard, but the actual amount was entirely at the discretion of whoever hired them. The workers themselves were in no position to negotiate. The Prodigal's experience as a swineherd illustrates how difficult life could be for workers who found themselves on that bottom rung of the economic ladder. Usually, there was simply no way up from there.

So hired servants were the poorest of the poor. But the Old Testament law had a provision that protected hired servants: "The wages of him who is hired shall not remain with you all night until morning" (Leviticus 19:13). Anyone who engaged the services of a day laborer was supposed to pay the worker his wages that very day. Because such workers needed everything they could possibly earn just to scrape by from day to day, it was considered unjust to withhold their wages until a scheduled payday at the end of the week or even later in the month. As the Prodigal's own experience demonstrated, not everyone paid menial workers enough to live on, and outside Israel (where Leviticus 19:13 did not apply), they might not get paid in a timely fashion.

But the Prodigal remembered that his father paid even the lowest of his hired servants more than enough. Day laborers who served his father actually had leftover food. That confirms what we have already observed about the father's character. He was generous, kindly, and compassionate. He regularly showed kindness to people by doing not only the minimum of what the Old Testament law and social custom required but even more.

That reality finally came home in the son's mind. Caught in a truly hard dilemma, he suddenly realized his father was not a hard man at all. Nor was his father even an indifferent man. He was kind, generous, good, and merciful.

A NEW PERSPECTIVE

We're reminded once again that the Prodigal Son was suddenly seeing *everything* in a fresh, new light, realizing for the very first time some vital truths he had never stopped to see before. Having lived all those years with a shallow, materialistic, self-centered worldview, he apparently had never even noticed or considered the reality that his father treated hired workers so well. He had never truly appreciated his father before. But a taste of reality had given him a whole new perspective. In all his travels and consorting with people who shared his worldly values, he had never met another person as kindly and generous as his father.

The pleasure-seeking lifestyle simply isn't conducive to values like compassion, generosity, and kindness. That is the harsh reality of life in the real world—even to this day.

An outside observer might think, *Wait a minute. This youth has totally disgraced and dishonored his father in the eyes of his own village. It would be folly to assume he could count on his father's mercy. Who cares if the father is a kind man? He must be furious with his wayward son. This father has been shamed by his own son, and he has shamed himself by giving in to the boy's original demands. Here's an opportunity to recover some honor by punishing the boy severely.* There's no question that's what the Pharisees would be thinking. They certainly would not have showed this wayward youth any mercy.

But the Prodigal knew his father better than that. He seems to have had little fear that his father would be vengeful toward him. He knew his father to be merciful, even if he had never consciously thought about it before. And now, left with no other

> Now, left with no other alternative, he was finally ready to go back home.

alternative, he was finally ready to go back home.

This is the nature of repentance as it is described in Scripture. The Greek word for repentance throughout the New Testament is *metanoia*, and its literal meaning speaks of a change of mind—a reversal in one's thinking. But the way the expression is employed throughout Scripture makes clear that repentance is much more than a simple or superficial change of opinion about something. It involves a whole new way of looking at life—a fundamental worldview change.

Sometimes theologians have disputed over questions such as whether repentance speaks of a change of opinion about God, a conscious repudiation of sin, or (as I heard one well-known teacher suggest) a simple change of belief about who Jesus really is. Actually, authentic repentance involves *all* those things. It's not a trite or temporary mood shift but a powerful, penetrating, soul-shattering, life-altering, attitude-changing, wholesale U-turn. It is the fruit of God's regenerating work, which Scripture portrays as the implantation of an entirely new heart and spirit (Ezekiel 11:19–20).

You can see evidence of genuine repentance in the Prodigal's very first thoughts after he finally came to himself. Those thoughts are seedlings that will bear abundant fruit over the long term—if they are planted in good soil. The Prodigal's heart, now made fallow by the harrowing consequences of his sin, was evidently good soil. Notice that his attitude toward his father was different. His willingness to acknowledge his own sin was brand-new. His will was changed. He was a markedly different man, from the inside out.

Therefore he was finally willing to humble himself, admit his terrible sin, own his shame, face the father whom he had so profoundly sinned against, and reenter the community where he had disgraced his own name so badly.

REACTIONS TO THE PRODIGAL'S CHANGE OF HEART

This parable, as we have seen, was tailor-made for Middle Eastern agrarian culture. Jesus' audience understood the imagery clearly and knew that the Prodigal Son had got himself into a mess from which there seemed to be no earthly way of escape. So all of them would be profoundly moved by the Prodigal's change of heart—although in different ways.

On the one hand, those who understood and identified with the youth's dilemma—people who were likewise sin-sick, discouraged, and longing to get out of whatever pigsty their lives had become—would find a ray of hope in his turnaround. Their ears would perk up to see whether the Prodigal would find redemption. Or was he already hopelessly beyond the point of no return? Jesus had deliberately framed the plot so that it might well seem that way.

On the other hand, those who listened through the filter of a Pharisaical worldview had already written the boy off completely. In their view, there was simply no way back from the disgrace and degradation into which he had sunk. Such sin, in their estimation, was so permanently defiling as to be (for all practical purposes) unforgivable. That was, after all, the very reason they objected to Jesus' habit of ministering to tax collectors and other outcasts. If any Pharisees in the audience believed there was even the hint of a possibility that the Prodigal could ever find forgiveness, they were certain that it could come only after a long, arduous time of hard work and penance for the sake of *earning* his father's pardon.

Actually, that would likely be the common assumption of everyone listening to Jesus as he told this parable. From the most devout Pharisees to the most desperate sinners (particularly those hoping to find some kind of deliverance for themselves), virtually all Jesus' hearers would share this one common presupposition: if the Prodigal had any hope of redemption whatsoever, it lay in a lifetime of hard work to atone for his misdeeds.

> Virtually all Jesus' hearers would share this one common presupposition: if the Prodigal had any hope of redemption whatsoever, it lay in a lifetime of hard work to atone for his misdeeds.

In other words, all Jesus' listeners would intuitively understand the Prodigal Son's planned course of action. He was thinking the way anyone in that culture would think. Family honor was a very serious matter, and someone who had disgraced his father like that frankly deserved to be treated as a dead man—utterly disowned, forgotten, his very existence denied.

Everyone fully understood that if the son were truly repentant, he would need to come crawling back to the father as a beggar. He would have to express his repentance verbally, be severely humiliated and scorned, shoulder all the public shame he had subjected his family to, and do everything he could to make restitution. In that culture, where honor and shame meant so much, such things were simply understood. It was the only way to restore the honor of the father. It was the only way for the son to regain any shred of dignity. That's what the boy needed to do, and that is just what he planned to do.

He was ready. He was broken. He was alone. He was downcast. He was penitent. He believed in his father.

As a matter of fact, this is a wonderful picture of the repentance that accompanies salvation—because of the way his repentance is inextricably bound up with faith in his father. He trusts in his father's mercy. Penitence therefore draws the Prodigal's heart and thoughts back to the father, rather than sending him fleeing even farther away. That is precisely what makes the difference between mere remorse and authentic, saving repentance.

THINKING THINGS THROUGH

Far from a mere mind change or an intellectual exercise, genuine repentance always demonstrates itself in the brokenness of the sinner's self-will. The sinner who has desperately tried to hide from God now diligently seeks Him instead. Apart from this quality, all the sorrow in the world is just meaningless remorse.

> Far from a mere mind change or an intellectual exercise, genuine repentance always demonstrates itself in the brokenness of the sinner's self-will.

Recall, for example, that Esau regretted selling his birthright, and he wept bitterly while pleading to get it back (Hebrews 12:17). That was not authentic repentance. Judas confessed that his treachery was wrong, returned the money he got for betraying Christ—and then went out and hanged himself (Matthew 27:3–5). That wasn't real repentance either.

David, on the other hand, in Psalm 51, fled directly into God's presence and pleaded, "Do not cast me away from Your presence, And do not take Your Holy Spirit from me" (v. 11). D. Martyn Lloyd-Jones, commenting on that passage, wrote,

> I do not hesitate to assert that this is perhaps the most subtle and delicate test as to whether we have repented, or where we are: our attitude towards God. Have you noticed it in the psalm? The one against whom David has sinned is God, and yet the one he desires above all is God. That is the difference between remorse and repentance. The man who has not repented, but who is only experiencing remorse, when he realizes he has done something against God, avoids God. . . . The man who has not been dealt with by the Spirit

of God and has not been convinced and convicted, tries to get away from God, to avoid him at all costs. He does not think, he does not read the Bible, he does not pray; he does everything he can not to think about these things. But the extraordinary thing about the man who is convicted of sin by the Holy Spirit is that though he knows he has sinned against God, it is God he wants—"Be merciful to me, O God." He wants to be with God—that is the peculiar paradox of repentance, wanting the one I have offended![1]

That is how repentance works. First of all, the sinner comes to himself and to his senses. He begins to look at reality and assess where he is. He realizes he is headed inevitably toward death and destruction and eternal damnation. He cannot keep going the same direction, so he turns to the Father, whom he has dishonored. Having spent a lifetime hiding, he now wants only to be in the Father's presence. He is therefore willing to acknowledge his own guilt and bear the shame of it. He is willing to do anything he can possibly do to honor the One he has so dishonored.

But something *also* tells him he can cast himself on the Father's mercy, forgiveness, and love—and find some measure of acceptance. This is the flip side of true repentance, and it's the very essence of saving faith.

The follow-through for the Prodigal Son's repentance would be humbling, embarrassing, even shameful. There's an element of that in any kind of repentance. But that doesn't matter to those who are truly penitent.

You see the evidence of that spirit in the Prodigal's own self-indictment as he planned his return: "I have sinned against heaven and before you" (Luke 15:18). The Greek expression literally speaks of sinning "*into* heaven." It may well suggest that he thought of his sins as a massive pile of guilt like a mountain, ascending toward heaven.

This could be an echo of Ezra 9:6: "O my God, I am too ashamed and humiliated to lift up my face to You, my God; for our iniquities have risen higher than our heads, and our guilt has grown up to the heavens." He was not holding anything back. This was authentic repentance, as evidenced by such full self-denial. His entire life had been a total disaster, and now—facing death, and with no one but himself to blame—he was repudiating it all. That's what self-denial means, in the sense Jesus called for it: "If anyone desires to come after Me, let him deny himself" (Luke 9:23).

There was no question of *whether* he should go home or not. He had reached the point where the only way he could survive was by turning back to the father he had spurned. His only thoughts now were about *how* to do it.

I love the way the Prodigal rehearsed how best to verbalize his repentance. It proves that when he *said* he was taking responsibility for his own wrongdoing, he meant it. He had thought this thing through. He had no expectations, asked for no special privileges, and made no demands. He wasn't negotiating terms of surrender. He fully and unconditionally relinquished all his rights. He simply confessed his sin, threw himself on his father's mercy, and begged to be made the lowest of servants.

Did he really think he could legitimately earn his way back into favor with his father? Whether he really thought he could or not, he needed to *try*. That's how people were taught to think by the religious culture of Jesus' day. Of course, he was hoping for some mercy. But he was *willing* to do whatever he could toward making restitution.

He was in the same situation as the servant in the parable of Matthew 18:22–35, who owed a debt of "ten thousand talents" (v. 24)—an incomprehensible amount, far more than the national debt of a country the size of Israel in those days. (How much was it? In 2 Kings 18:14, Sennacherib demanded tribute from King Hezekiah in the amount of "thirty talents of gold." Best estimates suggest thirty talents probably added up to some seventy pounds of gold. Ten thousand talents would therefore be more than 11.6

tons of gold!) That was an enormous personal debt, an utterly impossible amount for any servant to earn by working for it. Yet the servant begged to be permitted to try. He fell on his face in front of the master and pleaded, "Master, have patience with me, and I will pay you all" (Matthew 18:26). And the master had mercy and simply forgave him.

The Prodigal Son was in a similar position. There was no way he could ever make full restitution. But he was nevertheless willing to sacrifice everything for the rest of his life to do whatever he could.

The Pharisees and virtually everyone else in the crowd understood exactly what the young man was thinking. It was just what *had* to be done. The Pharisees' doctrine was based on working to earn divine favor. The Prodigal Son was penitent, and he trusted his father enough to come back home. But as far as the Pharisees were concerned, that was not going to be enough. He still needed to earn his way back into the father's good graces. That's pure Pharisaic theology. (It's also essentially what every man-made religion in the world teaches.)

> They had no concept of a mercy so great that the Father would grant full forgiveness and instant reconciliation before the sinner ever even performed a single work.

Most of the people in Jesus' audience likewise thought in those terms. If they thought of God's role in redemption at all, they regarded His grace only as a merciful supplement to whatever effort the sinner himself could put forth to secure favor. They had no concept of a mercy so great that the Father would grant full forgiveness and instant reconciliation before the sinner ever even performed a single work. Jesus' parable was about to explode their entire worldview.

CARRYING OUT THE PLAN

One clear indication that the Prodigal Son's repentance was genuine is seen in the simple fact that he followed through with what he told himself he would do. "He arose and came to his father" (Luke 15:20). His plans were not like a halfhearted New Year's resolution he would keep only if as long as it was convenient to do so. His "I will . . ." was a true expression of a whole new intention. Apparently he fulfilled his promise immediately, without hesitation. That's another factor that separates authentic repentance from mere regret.

It was not enough for the Prodigal Son to say, "I have sinned" (and merely wallow in his own despair) while remaining in the far country. He needed to go to his father and make that confession directly to the one he had wronged. That was the ultimate proof his repentance was genuine, and there would be no change in his circumstances until he followed through with that aspect of it.

So by whatever means he could, the Prodigal made his way back from the far country. No details are given about *how* he managed the journey. That aspect of the story was only incidental. But it's worth considering briefly that the Prodigal's trek home would have been totally different—and a thousand times more difficult—than his original outbound adventure into the far country. This time he was totally without resources, his energy was spent, his heart was broken, he was utterly friendless, and he was quite literally on the verge of death by starvation. It could not have been an easy expedition.

But the younger son remained single-mindedly devoted to fulfilling his repentance. We know this because, when he arrived at home and his father met him, he immediately began to articulate the confession he had rehearsed—verbatim. Those words reflect, then, what was truly on his heart. This was no halfhearted performance contrived to trick the father. It was deep, authentic, heartfelt repentance.

Furthermore, he came directly to the father, and not to an intermediary. He didn't need a go-between. Again, he's not negotiating terms of surrender. He wasn't going to pretend his failure was partly his father's fault and then treat the matter as a personal dispute that needed to be resolved through intervention, arbitration, or mediation. He was acknowledging without conditions and without reservations that he had wronged his father—and was then throwing himself on the father's mercy.

> Consider this: of all the iniquities the Prodigal had indulged in, the one sin with the most potential for evil was the great distance he had put between him and his father.

Consider this: of all the iniquities the Prodigal had indulged in, the one sin with the most potential for evil was the great distance he had put between him and his father. He was determined to remedy that transgression first of all. Everything else would come in its time.

He truly was seeing things more clearly now. No point in dragging it out. No need to meditate on the plan any longer. Now was the time to act. "And he arose and came to his father" (v. 20).

The Prodigal was at last going home.

PART 3

The Father

But when he was still a great way off, his father saw him and had compassion, and ran and fell on his neck and kissed him. And the son said to him, "Father, I have sinned against heaven and in your sight, and am no longer worthy to be called your son." But the father said to his servants, "Bring out the best robe and put it on him, and put a ring on his hand and sandals on his feet. And bring the fatted calf here and kill it, and let us eat and be merry; for this my son was dead and is alive again; he was lost and is found." And they began to be merry.

—Luke 15:20–24

❦ SEVEN ❧

His Forgiveness

When he was still a great way off, his father saw him and had compassion,
and ran and fell on his neck and kissed him.

—Luke 15:20

THE SCRIBES AND PHARISEES SURELY EXPECTED THE PRO-
digal Son's father to drop the hammer hard on the wayward youth.
After all, the father's honor had been turned to shame by his son's
rebellion, and the father had further brought shame on himself by
the lenient way he responded to the boy at the start. Hopefully this
father had learned a lesson even more valuable than whatever
practical wisdom the Prodigal had gained from his experiences.
Any father with a proper concern about the honor of his own
name and the reputation of the family would now see to it that a
boy like this received the full and just deserts of all his transgressions, right?

Bear in mind that Jesus was telling this parable chiefly for the
benefit of the scribes and Pharisees. In a story filled with shame
and shock and surprises, they were nevertheless on board with
Him up to here. Oh, yes—they were greatly amazed and even skep-
tical at the part about the Prodigal's repentance. But they definitely would affirm the boy's planned course of action: going
home, humbling himself, confessing that he had been wrong,
renouncing all rights to his position as a son, and working as a

hired servant in an outcast's role while he labored to make restitution. All of that, by their way of thinking, was exactly what the wayward youth needed to do. *Finally, some sanity in this story!*

THE PHARISEES' PERSPECTIVE SO FAR

The gross improprieties of the Prodigal Son's early behavior remained a large, almost impassible obstacle, preventing the Pharisees from showing him any empathy or compassion. They simply couldn't hear about such shameful behavior without being demonstratively and permanently offended. Their worldview demanded it. The very thought of that kind of sin was so utterly distasteful to them that for all practical purposes, they treated it as unforgivable. Their carefully maintained public veneer was, after all, designed to show contempt for everything embodied in the Prodigal's self-defilement: rebellion, worldliness, and other overt forms of conspicuous misbehavior. For them, when someone like that expressed any kind of repentance, even that was an occasion for scorn. They certainly had no category in their theology for showing grace to such a sinner.

So now that the boy was coming home, the Pharisees expected him to get what he deserved. The only question was how and how much the father would punish the boy—to save his own honor, and to shame the son in the way he deserved. Here was the part of the story that most captivated and appealed to their legalistic minds. By now they were engrossed.

One thing they were certain of: there could be no *instant* forgiveness. Nor was the Prodigal likely to merit *full* reconciliation with his father, ever. If the rebel wanted to come back home now, he would simply have to take his medicine in full doses.

In the Pharisees' idea of a best-case scenario, the chastened son would be excluded from fellowship in his family. He would probably live as a pariah on the outskirts of his father's estate, shouldering the futile burden of trying to repay his debt to the father for the rest of his life. That, after all, was merciful in the extreme—especially compared to what justice demanded (Deuteronomy 28:18–21).

Under such an arrangement, the boy could earn a decent salary and even have a permanent place to live in the servants' quarters—job security and a livable wage. He would no longer face the daily threat of starvation. But that was it. He would enjoy no special privileges. Not only could he never be a son again, but he would have no status at all. Why should he? *He* was the one who had renounced his own heritage and chose to live like a Gentile. In doing that, he forfeited forever all the rights that were his in his father's household. He could have no further share in his father's estate. After all, he had already received his full inheritance, liquidated it for much less than its value, and squandered it away. Remember, if the father followed social conventions, he would already have punctuated the Prodigal's renunciation of his own family with finality by having a funeral for the boy shortly after he had left home.

So as far as the Pharisees were concerned, the Prodigal was already dead to his father. He could consider himself fortunate indeed if the father even agreed to his request that he hire him as a common laborer. That was all mercy demanded, and it was the best option the penitent son could ever hope for. But he would still have to do a lifetime of hard labor in a hired servant's role. That's just how such things were supposed to be handled.

So what happened next was a seismic jolt to the Pharisees' worldview. Their eyes would roll and their heads would shake with shock and outrage at the reception the father gave the Prodigal Son.

WHAT EVERYONE EXPECTED

As the Prodigal Son approached his father's home, the reality and urgency of his situation must have been at the forefront of all his thinking. His life was now completely dependent on the mercy of his father. Without the father's resources, he would have no hope whatsoever. Everyone else in the village would certainly scorn him; people *had* to do that to protect their own honor. The Prodigal therefore hung helpless in the balance between life and death, and if his father turned him away, he would be doomed. In that culture, no one would even think of taking him in if his own father declared him an outcast. So *everything* hinged on his father's response.

> His entire future was now completely dependent on the mercy of his father.

As he drew nearer to his home, the Prodigal must have rehearsed his plea dozens, maybe hundreds, of times: "Father, I have sinned against heaven and before you, and I am no longer worthy to be called your son. Make me like one of your hired ser-vants" (Luke 15:18–19).

Perhaps he wondered how that request would sound to reasonable minds. *Was it outrageous for him to seek his father's mercy? Was he asking too much to ask for any favor at all?* That's how the typical person in that culture might feel. That's certainly how the Pharisees saw it. The Prodigal's conscience would be scourging him with reminders of all the foolish and wicked things he had done that dishonored his father. Who was he to ask for help now—especially since he had already been given so much and squandered it all and thus had nothing left of any real value to offer in return for his father's kindness? What if the father took his plea for mercy as just another scandalous request and turned him away forever?

In that culture of honor, especially in a situation like this, it would be nothing extraordinary if the father simply refused to meet the boy face-to-face. In fact, even if the father were inclined to grant the penitent son an audience, it would be fairly typical to punish him first by making a public spectacle of his shame. For example, a father in those circumstances might have the son sit outside the gate in public view for several days, letting him soak up some of the dishonor he had brought upon his own family. The boy would be completely exposed to the elements—and worse, to the utter derision of the whole community.

You see, in a typical village where everyone knew everyone else, the significance of such a gesture from the father would be instantly understood by all. If a father denied his own son an immediate face-to-face meeting and made him sit in the public square instead, the entire village would treat the boy with utter scorn—mocking and verbally abusing him and possibly even spitting on him. Less privileged people in the community would go out of their way to show their disdain for this boy who had been blessed with every advantage and had thrown it all away. No indignity would be too great to heap on his head. He would just have to sit there and take it while he waited.

That may seem harsh, but remember—the full penalty prescribed by Moses' law for such a rebellious son was death by public stoning. The instructions in the law ordered that "all the men of his city shall stone him to death with stones; so you shall put away the evil from among you" (Deuteronomy 21:21). So public humiliation in lieu of stoning was actually a mercy the boy did not deserve. And in that culture where honor and shame meant so much, the community's profound contempt for this boy's behavior practically demanded some kind of expression.

Most likely, that's precisely the kind of treatment the Prodigal Son expected. It was the cost of readmission to the village he himself had shunned. It was just one phase of a long process he would need to be prepared to endure. If the Prodigal had counted the cost of repentance, such treatment should not even take him by surprise. By the social customs of that culture, having been the cause of so much shame, he now *needed* to be shamed by everyone else, as a vital part of the just retribution he deserved. He had made himself a pariah; he'd have to expect to be treated like one.

After a few days' wait like that, if the father did decide to grant him an audience—assuming he was willing to extend a measure of mercy to the penitent rebel—the son would be expected to bow low and kiss the father's feet. No embrace. It would not even be right for him to stand and kiss his father's hand. The only proper demeanor for such a son would be to fall prostrate with his face to the ground before the father whom he had disgraced.

The father would most likely meet him with a measure of frigid indifference. To save face, the father would need to approach the arrangement formally, like a business deal, without showing any overt affection or tenderness for the boy. There was no negotiation to be done; the father would simply outline the terms of employment—spelling out what would be required of the boy, what kind of labor he could expect to be assigned, and how long he needed to serve before he could be given even the smallest measure of privilege.

An Old Testament Parallel:
Joseph and His Brothers

We see an interesting parallel to this situation in the Old Testament account of Joseph's reconciliation with his brothers. The story should be familiar to most—how the brothers sold Joseph into slavery, and yet he famously rose despite every conceivable trial and setback to become the second most powerful man in Egypt.

Years later, when the brothers were forced by a famine to go into Egypt to seek relief, they encountered Joseph without realizing who he was. At first (until he learned from them the whereabouts of their father and youngest brother), Joseph used a stern, even threatening, demeanor with them. He had no intention of harming them, of course. But to elicit their cooperation and complete honesty—and perhaps to discover whether they were the least bit remorseful for their sin against him—Joseph used his authority to good advantage. He made his brothers sweat (over a period of several days or weeks, it seems) until he was ready to reveal who he was and assure his brothers of his forgiveness.

Of course, Joseph had no duty to show his brothers that kind of favor, and he had every right to punish them for what they had done to him. They knew it too. Even after Joseph revealed his true identity and welcomed them with tears, they still feared what he might do. When their father, Jacob, died, they thought Joseph might decide to seek revenge. So they offered to be made his servants (Genesis 50:18). Joseph then made it absolutely clear that he forgave them completely and unconditionally.

But Joseph's forgiveness toward his brothers was an extraordinary, otherworldly, one-of-a-kind act from one of the most renowned figures in Israel's history. No one would expect anything like that from the Prodigal's father—not the Prodigal Son himself, not the villagers in his father's community, not his elder brother, not the people in Jesus' audience, and certainly not the Pharisees.

HOW THE PLOT SHIFTED

At this point, Jesus' parable suddenly took another dramatic and unexpected turn. Here was a father not merely willing to grant a measure of mercy in return for the promise of a lifetime of meritorious service—but *eager* to forgive freely, completely, at the very first sign of repentance: "When he was still a great way off, his father saw him and had compassion, and ran and fell on his neck and kissed him" (Luke 15:20).

It is evident that the father was looking diligently for the Prodigal's return. How else could he have seen him while he was still a long way off? We can safely imagine that the father had been looking steadily, scanning the horizon daily, repeatedly, for signs of the boy's return. He had been at it a long time too—probably since long before the initial shock of the boy's departure had even worn off.

Obviously, the heartache had not yet worn off, because the father was still watching. And he kept watching daily, heartbroken but hopeful, privately bearing the unspeakable pain of suffering love for his son. He surely knew that the kind of life his son was headed for would eventually end up the way it did. He desperately hoped the boy would survive and come back home. So he filled his spare time watching expectantly. He must have gone to the highest point on his property—perhaps on a tower or rooftop—and spent his idle moments scanning the horizon, praying for the boy's safe return, and thinking about what it would be like when and if the Prodigal returned. A man such as this father would probably have turned that scenario over in his own mind countless times.

It was daylight when the father finally spotted the wayward boy. (We know that detail because it's the only way he could have seen him "a great way off.") That meant the village center was full of people. The markets were busy with merchants selling, people buying, women with children, and older people sitting in the public square while they watched the bustling activity. The moment the son approached the village, someone would no doubt recognize him and shout the news of his return. Someone else would likely run to tell the father about it.

So why was the father watching? And why did he run to the son rather than waiting for the son to come to him? First, and most obviously, the father was truly eager to initiate forgiveness and reconciliation with his son. That aspect of this parable echoes the previous two parables, where the shepherd diligently sought his lost sheep and the woman feverishly searched for her lost coin. Each of those images pictures Christ as the faithful Seeker. He is the architect and the initiator

> The father was truly eager to initiate forgiveness and reconciliation with his son.

of our salvation. He seeks and draws sinners to Himself before they ever would think of seeking Him. He always makes the first overture. He Himself pays the redemption-price. He calls, justifies, sanctifies and finally glorifies each believing sinner (Romans 8:30). Every aspect of our salvation is His gracious work.

This imagery of the father running to meet the Prodigal Son fills in the details of the big picture even more. It illustrates the truth that God is slow to anger and swift to forgive. He has no pleasure in the death of the wicked but is eager, willing, even *delighted* to save sinners.

What Was the Father Thinking?

There's a second major factor at play here, however. The father clearly wanted to reach the Prodigal before the boy reached the village—apparently to protect him from the outpouring of scorn and invective he would surely receive if he walked through that village unreconciled with his father. The father himself would bear the shame and take the abuse instead.

And make no mistake: in the context of that culture, the father's action of running to the boy and embracing him before he even came all the way home was seen as a shameful breech of decorum. In the jaded perspective of the scribes and Pharisees, this was just one more thing that added to the father's shame. For one thing, noblemen in that culture did not run. Running was for little boys and servants. Grown men did not run—especially men of dignity and importance. They walked magisterially, with a slow gait and deliberate steps. But Jesus says "his father . . . *ran*" (v. 20; emphasis added). He did not send a servant or a messenger ahead to intercept his son. And it was not merely that he quickened his pace. *He himself ran.* The text uses a word that speaks of sprinting, as if he were in an athletic competition. The father gathered up the hem of his robe and took off in a most undignified manner.

The image of a respectable, wealthy, honorable man such as this running seems so out of place in Middle Eastern culture that Arabic Bible translators have traditionally been reluctant to translate the phrase without resorting to a euphemism such as "he hurried," or "he presented himself." Kenneth E. Bailey, an evangelical Bible commentator who lived in the Middle East and made careful studies of the language and culture there, wrote:

> The reluctance on the part of the Arabic versions to let the father run is amazing. . . . For a thousand years a wide range of such phrases were employed (almost as if there was a conspiracy) to avoid the humiliating truth of the text—the father *ran*! The explanation for all of this is simple. The tradition identified the father with God, and running in public is too humiliating to attribute to a person who symbolizes God. Not until 1860, with the appearance of the Bustani–Van Dyck Arabic Bible, does the father appear running. The work sheets of the translators are available to me and even in that great version the first rendition of the Greek was "he hurried," and only in the second round of the translation process does *rakada* (he ran) appear. The Hebrew of Prov. 19:2 reads, "He that hastens with his feet sins" (my translation). The father represents God. How could he *run?* He does.[1]

The father was humbling himself, even though the Prodigal Son was the one who should have been doing so.

Most of us today would see this moment when the father ran to embrace his son as the most poignant, tender moment in the parable. It was certainly not viewed that way by the Pharisees. Nor would the typical listener in Jesus' audience simply take it in stride and admire the father's compassion. This was a scandal. It was shocking. It was even more offensive to them than the sins of the Prodigal.

But the father was nevertheless willing to have the villagers whisper among themselves, "What does he think he is doing? This boy took advantage of his father and sinned horribly against him. The boy should be made an outcast. Instead, this man who was dishonored by his own son now dishonors himself even more by embracing the wretched boy!" The father in effect positioned himself between his son and all the scorn, taunting, and abuse people in that culture would naturally have heaped on the boy's head.

Our version says the father "had compassion" (v. 20), but the Greek expression is even more emphatic. It uses a word that literally speaks of a sensation in the viscera—or in today's vernacular, a gut feeling. The father was powerfully moved with compassion, an emotion so deep and so forceful that it made his stomach churn.

The father's compassion was not merely sorrow over his son's past sin. Nor was it only a momentary sympathy prompted by the boy's present filthiness. (Remember, the Prodigal was by now in rags and smelled like pigs.) Certainly the father's feeling toward the son included a deep sense of pity over all the terrible things sin had already done to him. But it seems obvious that something else was amplifying the father's anguish at that precise moment. His action of running toward the son and intercepting him on the road suggests he had something terribly urgent and immediate on his mind. That's why I am convinced that what moved the father to run was a deep sense of empathy in anticipation of the contempt that was sure to be poured on the son as he walked through the village. The father took off in a sprint in order to be the first person to reach him, so that he could deflect the abuse he knew the boy would suffer.

> The father took off in a sprint in order to be the first person to reach him, so that he could deflect the abuse he knew the boy would suffer.

This is indeed a fitting picture of Christ, who humbled Himself to seek and to save the lost—and then "endured the cross, despising the shame" (Hebrews 12:2). Like this father, He willingly took upon Himself all the bitter scorn, the contempt, the mockery, and the wrath our sin fully deserves. He even took our guilt upon His own innocent shoulders. He bore everything for our sake and in our stead.

If the truth were known, this father's behavior, undignified as it might have seemed to Jesus' audience, was actually nothing very remarkable compared to the amazing grace unveiled in the incarnation and death of Christ. As a matter of fact, that was one of the key lessons Jesus was challenging the Pharisees with through His tale.

An Amazing Display of Grace

When the father reached the wayward son, he couldn't contain his affection, and he didn't hesitate in granting forgiveness. This was even more shocking to the Pharisees than the imagery of a grown man sprinting down a dusty road to greet a derelict son.

The father immediately embraced the Prodigal. Jesus said the father "fell on his neck and kissed him" (v. 20). The verb tense means he kissed him repeatedly. He collapsed on the boy in a massive hug, buried his head in the neck of his son—stinking and dirty and unpresentable as he was—and welcomed him with a display of unbridled emotion.

It is evident that the father had been suffering in quiet grief the entire time the boy was gone. His deep love for the youth had never once wavered. The yearning to see him wise up and come home must have been a painful burning in the father's heart. It filled his thoughts every day. And now that he saw the bedraggled figure of his son alone on the horizon, it mattered little to the father what people thought of *him*; he was determined to welcome home the boy as personally and publicly as possible.

Furthermore, the father would spare the boy from any more of the reproach of his sin—by becoming a reproach himself. In essence, he took the boy's disgrace completely upon himself—emptying himself of all pride, renouncing his fatherly rights, not caring at all about his own honor (even in that culture, where honor seemed like everything). And in an amazing display of selfless love—openly despising the shame of it all (cf. Hebrews 12:2)—he opened his arms to the returning sinner and hugged him tightly in an embrace designed partly to shield him from any more humiliation. By the time the boy walked into the village, he was already fully reconciled to his father.

The Prodigal had come home prepared to kiss his Father's feet. Instead, the father was kissing the Prodigal's pig-stinking head. Such an embrace with repeated kisses was a gesture that signified not only the father's delirious joy but also his full acceptance, friendship, love, forgiveness, restoration, and total reconciliation. It was a deliberate and demonstrative way of signaling to the whole village that the father had fully forgiven his son, without any qualms or hesitancy.

What a beautiful picture this is of the forgiveness offered in the gospel! The typical sinner wants out of the morass of sin, and his first instinct is to devise a plan. He will work off his guilt. He will reform himself. But such a plan could never succeed. The debt is too great to repay, and the sinner is helpless to change his own status. He is fallen, and he cannot alter that fact. So the Savior intercepts him. Christ has already run the gauntlet, taken the shame for himself, suffered the rebukes, borne the cruel taunts, and paid the price of the guilt in full. He embraces the sinner, pours out love upon him, grants complete forgiveness, and reconciles him to God.

A Speech Interrupted

It is significant that the father was already granting forgiveness before the son said a word. After the father embraced him, the Prodigal started to make the confession he had been rehearsing:

"Father, I have sinned against heaven and in your sight, and am no longer worthy to be called your son." (Luke 15:21)—but he barely got that far and the father quickly cut him off, giving orders to the servants to begin preparations for a celebratory banquet.

The Prodigal never even got to the part of his rehearsed speech in which he would ask to become one of the hired servants. By the time he completed his first sentence, the father had already reinstated him as a beloved son, and the great celebration was under way.

The father seems to have perceived the depth and reality of the boy's repentance from the simple fact that the boy had come home. He knew his own son well enough to know what his return signified. He could tell from the boy's appalling condition how much he had suffered the cruel consequences of his sin. So he didn't even permit the boy to finish making his confession before he granted him mercy. This was an act of grace that went far, far beyond anything the boy had ever dared to hope for.

The boy had done nothing whatsoever to atone for his own sin, and yet the father's forgiveness was full and lavish anyway, with nothing held back.

The Prodigal's unfinished confession may seem a subtle detail in the parable, but it made a not-so-subtle point for the Pharisees' benefit. There was no way they could have failed to notice one glaring reality in Jesus' description of the father's eagerness to forgive. The boy had done nothing whatsoever to atone for his own sin, and yet the father's forgiveness was full and lavish anyway, with nothing held back.

As far as the Pharisees were concerned, this outpouring of love and forgiveness toward a flagrant and self-confessed sinner was radical and totally unorthodox. Doesn't common sense demand that sins be atoned for? Didn't God Himself say He will not justify the wicked (Exodus 23:7) and that He will by no means allow the guilty to go unpunished (Exodus 34:7)? How could a notorious rebel like the Prodigal Son simply be let off scot-free? Whatever happened to righteousness? What about the principles of divine justice? Wasn't the entire Old Testament system filled to overflowing with priests and sacrifices and other symbols of atonement—precisely in order to stress this fundamental truth?

THE NECESSITY OF ATONEMENT

It is quite true that sin *must* be atoned for. Don't imagine for a moment that when God forgives sin, He simply looks the other way and pretends the sin never occurred. Moses' law was filled with bloody sacrifices precisely to make that truth inescapable.

This point is crucial and ultimately pivotal in understanding the parable of the prodigal son. Remember that the main point Jesus was making in this parable was for the Pharisees' benefit. He was addressing their faulty idea about God—that He found joy in their self-righteousness rather than in the forgiveness of sins. Their theology was so lacking any sense of true grace that they simply could not account for how forgiven sinners might stand before God apart from a lifetime of religious effort. The Pharisees' misunderstanding about what is required to make full atonement for sin lay at the root of their errant theology.

Don't forget how the Pharisees had overlaid the truth of the Old Testament with their own elaborate system of human traditions, manmade rules, and useless ceremonies. They were convinced sinners needed to do good works to help atone for their own sins. They had even enshrined their own intricate system of finely detailed traditions as the *chief* means by which they thought it possible to acquire the kind of merit they believed would balance out the guilt of sin. That is why they were obsessed with ostentatious works, religious rituals, spiritual stunts, ceremonial displays of righteousness, and other external and cosmetic achievements. And they clung doggedly to that system, even though most of their rituals were nothing more than their own inventions, designed to paper over sin and make them *appear* righteous.

Here was the problem with that: even *authentically* good works could never accomplish what the Pharisees hoped their ceremonial traditions would accomplish. That was made perfectly clear by the Law itself. The Law demanded no less than absolute perfection (Matthew 5:19, 48; James 2:10). And it was filled from start to finish with threats and curses against anyone who violated it at any point. The reason we need atonement is that we are fallen sinners who *cannot* keep the Law adequately. Why would anyone ever think to earn enough merit to atone for sin through an imperfect obedience to the Law? That was the fatal flaw in the Pharisees' system.

In fact, the Law itself made perfectly clear that the price of full atonement was more costly than any mere human could ever possibly pay: "The soul who sins shall die" (Ezekiel 18:4).

We Cannot Atone for Our Own Sin

Furthermore, and more to the point, the Old Testament never once suggested that sinners could atone for their own sin (either wholly or even in part) by doing good works or performing elaborate rituals. In fact, the dominant picture of atonement in the Old Testament is that of an innocent substitute whose blood was shed on behalf of the sinner.

The shedding of the substitute's blood was perhaps the single most prominent aspect of atonement for sin. "Without shedding of blood there is no remission" (Hebrews 9:22). On the Day of Atonement, the blood of the sin offering was deliberately splashed onto everything in the vicinity of the altar. The priest "sprinkled with blood both the tabernacle and all the vessels of the ministry. And according to the law almost all things are purified with blood"

(vv. 21–22)—the worshiper included. This was not to suggest that the blood itself had some kind of magical, mystical, or metaphysical property that literally washed away sin's defilement. But the purpose of this bloody ritual was simple: the blood everywhere made a vivid—and intentionally revolting— illustration of the fearsome reality that the wages of sin is death. "For the life of the flesh is in the blood, and I have given it to you upon the altar to make atonement for your souls; for it is the blood that makes atonement for the soul" (Leviticus 17:11).

By definition, then, no sinner can ever fully atone for his or her own sin, and that is why Scripture so frequently stresses the need for a substitute.

> By definition, then, no sinner can ever fully atone for his or her own sin, and that is why Scripture so frequently stresses the need for a substitute.

We Need a Substitute

When Abraham was told to sacrifice Isaac on an altar, for example, God Himself supplied a substitute in the form of a ram to be slain in Isaac's place. At Passover, the substitute was a spotless lamb. The main staple of the sacrificial system under Moses' law was the burnt offering, which could be a young bull, lamb, goat, turtledove, or pigeon (depending on the financial abilities of the worshiper). And once a year, on the Day of Atonement, the high priest sacrificed a bull and a goat, along with an additional burnt offering, as a symbol of atonement—a *substitute* who suffered for the sins of all the people.

Now it should be obvious to anyone that "it is not possible that the blood of bulls and goats could take away sins" (Hebrews 10:4; cf. Micah 6:6–8). That's why the ritual sacrifices had to be repeated daily. Everyone who ever seriously thought about the sacrificial system and weighed the real cost of sin had to face this truth eventually: animal sacrifices simply could not provide a full and final atonement for sin. Something more needed to be done to make a full atonement.

There were basically two possible answers to the dilemma. One approach was to adopt a system of merit such as the Pharisees' religion, in which the sinner himself tried to embellish or supplement the atoning significance of the animal sacrifices with several more layers of good works. In the Pharisees' case, this seems to be the very reason they made up their own long list of exacting rules and regulations that went so far beyond what the Law actually required. They knew very well that simple obedience to the Law couldn't possibly be perfect and therefore could never achieve enough merit to atone for sin. So they artificially supplemented what the Law required, thinking that their extra works would enable them to gain supplemental merit. The inevitable result was a system that promoted the most blatant forms of self-righteousness while diminishing the proper role of true faith.

The other approach was the one followed by every truly faithful person from the beginning of time until the coming of Christ. They acknowledged their own inability to atone for sin, embraced God's promise of forgiveness, and trusted Him to send a Redeemer who would provide a full and final atonement (Isaiah 59:20). From the day when Adam and Eve ate the forbidden fruit and their race was cursed, faithful believers had looked for the promised offspring of the woman who would finally crush the serpent's head and thus put sin and guilt away forever (Genesis 3:15). Despite some very strong hints (including Daniel 9:24 and Isaiah 53:10), the actual means by which redemption would finally be accomplished remained shrouded in mystery, until Jesus Himself explained it after His resurrection to some disciples on the road to Emmaus (Luke 24:27).

Notice that Jesus did not mention anything about the actual *means* of atonement in the parable of the prodigal son. That, after all, wasn't the point of the story. But our Lord did nevertheless directly confront the heart of the Pharisees' error, which was their insistence that all sinners need to perform certain works to atone for their own sin—and thus earn the forgiveness and favor of God.

THE ONLY WAY TO BE JUSTIFIED BEFORE GOD

The parable of the prodigal son debunks that false idea. It illustrates instead the simple truth of how and why repentant faith is the only means by which any sinner can find justification before God. Forgiveness is not a reward for merits we earn by good works. Don't imagine, however, that practical righteousness is eliminated altogether—because good works are the inevitable fruit of faith. But sinners who repent and turn to God are fully and instantly justified, freely forgiven from the first moment of faith's inception—before a single good work is done.

> Repentant faith is the only means by which any sinner can find justification before God.

That was the principal lesson of Abraham's example. "He *believed* in the LORD, and He accounted it to him for righteousness" (Genesis 15:6; emphasis added). His faith was the sole means by which he laid hold of God's promises. In Romans 4, Paul makes an extended argument showing that David was likewise justified though faith alone, rather than through the performance of any good deeds, religious rituals, or meritorious works designed to nullify the debt of sin.

In a similar way, the Prodigal Son is a textbook example of someone who is justified by grace through faith apart from meritorious deeds. His forgiveness was a fully settled reality, and his status as a privileged son was established beyond question before he ever even had an opportunity to finish expressing his repentance.

That lifetime of work he was prepared to offer as a servant to his father? It was utterly unnecessary as a means of earning the father's favor. The father had granted his full blessing and unconditional pardon by grace alone.

But this repentant young man would nevertheless be permanently changed because of the grace his father showed him. Why would he ever go back to a life of self-indulgence and prodigality? He had already pursued sin to its inevitable end and knew the results all too well. He was severely chastened by the bitterness of that experience. He had drunk the awful dregs of sin's consequences.

But now the blinders had been taken from his eyes. He saw his father in a new light, and he loved him with a new appreciation. He had every reason henceforth to remain faithful. He would be serving his father now with gladness—not as a hired servant but with the full status of a beloved son.

EIGHT

His Generosity

The father said to his servants, "Bring out the best robe and put it on him, and put a ring on his hand and sandals on his feet. And bring the fatted calf here and kill it, and let us eat and be merry; for this my son was dead and is alive again; he was lost and is found."

—Luke 15:22–24

IMAGINE WHAT THE SCENARIO SURROUNDING THE Prodigal's return looked like from the perspective of one of the household servants. The father suddenly came hurrying down from his watch post. He blew past his own servants, dashed out the front gate, and went running down the dusty road with his robes held up high past his knees. He shot through town without slowing down and without regard to who might be watching. Behind him trailed several servants who would be sprinting to keep up with their master, but with no clue about where he was going or why he was running like that.

The scene probably looked comical to some, but it would not have been funny to his servants. They would find his behavior shameful. It was out of character, disturbing, even frightening. They had no choice but to come along because, as servants from his household, this was their duty.

The servants must have watched in amazement as their master reached his son, embraced him (stinking, pig-slop-stained rags and

125

all), and started kissing him as if the boy were a returning hero. Then, almost before the servants could collect their senses, the father looked up, turned to the servants (who were likely huffing and puffing from their sprint), and sent them on a series of urgent errands. The best Greek texts say he preceded his orders with the adverb *tachu*: "Quickly!" He wanted no delay. It was a matter of the utmost urgency to him, and everything needed to be done as speedily as possible.

As the father gave his orders, it became clear that he was going to hold a banquet for this son who had dishonored him so badly. He was planning to treat him the way someone might treat an honored dignitary—with gifts, a full celebration, and the ceremonial bestowal of high privileges.

Recall, now, that the word *prodigal* means extravagant. A prodigal person is a big spender who spreads his resources around, mostly for the purpose of merrymaking. The term conveys the idea of someone who is excessively lavish, imprudent in what he spends his money on, immoderate in the speed with which he burns through his assets, and recklessly openhanded with large gratuities.

Suddenly the father, not the wayward son, is the prodigal one: "The father said to his servants, 'Bring out the best robe and put it on him, and put a ring on his hand and sandals on his feet. And bring the fatted calf here and kill it, and let us eat and be merry; for this my son was dead and is alive again; he was lost and is found.' And they began to be merry" (Luke 15:22–24).

Here again, as Jesus told the story, eyes in his audience would roll. Not only the Pharisees, but anyone steeped in that culture would be utterly bewildered by the father's actions. This man had no shame. He had just sacrificed his last shred of dignity by running like a schoolboy to grant free and complete forgiveness to a son who deserved nothing more than the full weight of his father's wrath.

As if those actions weren't disgraceful enough, now the father was about to use the very best of everything he owned (and spend a lot of money in the process) to honor the dishonorable boy—who had already managed to sin away a considerable portion of the family's wealth in the far country. Even if the delinquent boy had truly repented, bestowing costly gifts on him and giving him such an extravagant celebration seemed exactly the wrong thing for this moment.

But the father, undeterred by fear of public opinion, wasted no time getting the party started. Even before the elder brother could be summoned from the fields, the father had called for a robe and a ring. The fatted calf was already being slaughtered for a great feast.

> Oblivious to his own reputation, the father was showering the Prodigal Son with honor after honor.

The stunned Prodigal Son must have felt his head spinning. After everything he had done—and everything sin had done to him—he would hardly be able to grasp what was happening. The villagers would likewise be completely baffled by the father's behavior. What was he doing? Oblivious to his own reputation, the father was showering the Prodigal Son with honor after honor. These were all staggeringly generous favors, which the boy by no means deserved.

REINSTATING HIS SON'S STATUS

Jesus mentions three gifts the father immediately gave his penitent son: a robe, a ring, and sandals. Everyone listening to Jesus' story understood the implications of those gifts.

Sandals—The Gift of Sonship

The sandals may sound like the least of the gifts, but they were highly significant. They made an unmistakable symbolic statement about the father's acceptance of his son. Hired servants and household slaves customarily went barefoot. Only masters and their sons wore footwear. So the shoes were an important gesture that signified the former rebel's full and immediate reinstatement as a privileged son. To anyone familiar with the culture, this was no small thing.

On a certain level, even in that culture, the father's great sense of gladness and relief was completely understandable. But the extravagance with which he forgave was not. If he wasn't willing to make the wayward boy work off part of his debt by consigning him to servitude, then that alone would have been an extraordinary, over-the-top act of kindness.

But surely before the father gave him any public honor like a costly banquet, he needed to take a more tentative approach. Shouldn't the father withhold *some* privileges—at least until the boy demonstrated how serious he was? Didn't he need to lay down some ground rules for the boy? Wasn't it fair to expect to see the fruits of his repentance? A year or two would not have been too long to ask such a boy to prove his faithfulness before granting him the full rights of a loyal adult son.

> The father's acceptance of his son is immediate and complete.

A sensible measure of restraint somewhere along the line would seem only prudent. But there's no hint of anything like that. The father's acceptance of his son is immediate and complete.

Robe—The Gift of Honor

The robe was an even higher honor. Every nobleman had a choice robe—an expensive, ornate, embroidered, one-of-a-kind, floor-length outer garment of the highest quality fabric and craftsmanship. It was a garment so special that he wouldn't even think of wearing it as a guest to someone else's wedding. It would be reserved instead for his own children's weddings or equivalent occasions. The closest twenty-first-century parallel might be an expensive tuxedo that stays in someone's closet except perhaps once a year (or less). Even in that culture, if you were invited to a very formal occasion and did not own a suitable garment, you might have to buy or rent one.

But every head of a well-to-do family in the first century owned a special robe like that. It was his most beautiful, finely crafted piece of formal wear. The Greek expression in Luke 15:22 literally means "first-ranking garment."

He wanted to put *that* on this reformed swineherd before the boy even had an opportunity to clean himself up? Everyone in the village would be aghast at such a thought. Giving him the robe signified a greater honor than one would normally even think to confer on a son. This was the kind of courtesy reserved for an extremely prestigious visiting dignitary. The father was publicly honoring his returning son not only as guest of honor at the banquet but also as a person of the utmost distinction.

Ring—The Gift of Authority

That's not all. The father also called for a ring to put on the boy's hand. This was a signet ring that had the family crest or seal, so when the ring was pressed into melted wax on a formal document, the resulting seal served as legal authentication. The ring therefore was a symbol of authority. Exactly how much and what kind of authority is a matter we shall shortly examine in more detail.

But for now, consider the big-picture significance of all this: the sandals, robe, and ring all belonged to the father and were symbols of his honor and authority. The father was also calling for the greatest celebration that had ever occurred in that family—perhaps the grandest banquet that village had ever seen. In giving the three gifts to his son, he was in effect telling him, "The best of all that I have is yours. You are now fully restored to sonship, and even elevated in our household to a position of honor. No longer are you a rebellious adolescent. Now you are a full-grown adult son, with all the privilege that comes with that position, and I want you to enjoy it fully." Like a king passing his robe and signet ring to a prince, the father did this ceremoniously and publicly, to eliminate any question from anyone's mind about whether he really meant it or not. This was yet another self-emptying act by the father.

Even in our culture, it is hard to conceive of any father taking forgiveness that far. But it is yet another proof that *this* father seems not to be the least bit concerned about his own honor in the eyes of the critics.

It is also a powerful reminder that the father here is a symbol of Christ, "who, although He existed in the form of God, did not regard equality with God a thing to be grasped, but emptied Himself, taking the form of a bond-servant, and being made in the likeness of men. Being found in appearance as a man, He humbled Himself by becoming obedient to the point of death, even death on a cross" (Philippians 2:6–8 NASB).

Notice that Christ emptied Himself not by ceasing to be God, and not by divesting himself of His divine nature or attributes, but by taking a real, authentic human nature on Himself and thereby covering His glory with the shroud of His humanity. He thus stepped down from His grandeur and majesty and became a man. He put himself on our level. Then He humbled Himself even further by suffering the most ignominious kind of death by capital punishment—as if He embodied all the worst traits of the lowest dregs of human society. That's what the phrase "even death on a cross" signifies. It's a far greater act of humiliation than any indignity the father in this parable suffered. So if the behavior of the father in the parable seems exaggerated, don't miss the fact that the disgrace the father bore could not possibly be exaggerated enough to even begin to be in the same league as the humility of Christ.

Moreover, the parable reminds us that Christ receives sinners who are in exactly the same situation as the Prodigal Son—unclean, clothed in filthy rags, utterly bereft of any assets, with nothing whatsoever to commend themselves to Christ. He receives them with the same kind of gladness seen in this parable—and infinitely more. In the words of Romans 4:5, Christ "justifies the ungodly." If that thought doesn't make you want to weep with gratitude, then you have probably never felt yourself in the place of the Prodigal Son, and you need to pray for repentance.

Of course, that was the very issue that put the scribes and Pharisees at odds with Christ. They refused to see Jesus' ministry of seeking and saving sinners as the activity of God. The idea that Jesus would receive filthy sinners was positively repugnant to them. It was beneath their notion of what the Messiah should be like. And the fact that He would justify sinners through faith alone and instantly treat them as if they had a perfect standing with God (cf. Luke 18:14) was simply more than the Pharisees could bear. After all, most of them had labored their whole lives at their religion, and Christ treated them with less deference than He showed to the tax collectors and other lowlifes who came to Him. In their minds, Jesus was defiled by those associations with sinners. The Pharisees had therefore convinced themselves that they were far more righteous—and therefore even more glorious—than He was.

> The parable reminds us that Christ receives sinners who are in exactly the same situation as the Prodigal Son . . . with the same kind of gladness seen in this parable—and infinitely more.

How badly they misunderstood what true glory looks like! Although Christ stepped down from His heavenly glory, He now inherits an even higher honor. As a matter of fact, His suffering and death (which soon would become the biggest stumbling block of all to people who thought like the Pharisees) put on display some of the greatest features of God's eternal glory: His loving grace and forgiveness.

Philippians 2 continues with this declaration: "Therefore God also has highly exalted Him and given Him the name which is above every name, that at the name of Jesus every knee should bow, of those in heaven, and of those on earth, and of those under the earth, and that every tongue should confess that Jesus Christ is Lord, to the glory of God the Father" (vv. 9–11).

RESTORING HIS SON'S PRIVILEGE

The ceremonial presentation of the three gifts was no mere sentimental gesture. The father was making a public declaration that carried profound and far-reaching legal weight. Just as the sandals signified that the Prodigal was to be a treated as a son rather than a hired servant, and the robe demonstrated that he was not merely a son but a highly favored one, the signet ring carried a meaning that everyone in that culture understood. It formally endowed the Prodigal Son with a legal right known as *usufruct*.

Those familiar with legal terminology—especially probate law—will immediately recognize that term. The legal principle of usufruct has a long history that goes back at least to early Roman law, and it is still a recognized right in most systems of civil law today. *Usufruct* is a Latin expression that literally means "use of the fruits," and it describes the legal right to use someone else's property or assets freely and reap the fruits of them as if they were one's own personal possessions.

In other words, usufruct confers all the rights of ownership without actually transferring the title of ownership per se. The usufructuary (the nonowner receiving this right) is not authorized to sell, damage, or diminish the value of the property in question. But beyond that, he is free to use it any way he likes. If it's a field, he can cultivate it and reap the profits of the venture without any obligation to pay rent. If it's real estate, he can use the property as if it were his own, or even lease it out to someone else and collect the proceeds for himself. This was a high and powerful privilege, similar to power of attorney, but specifically with respect to the use of property.

Don't forget that this family's assets had already been formally divided between the two sons (Luke 15:12). The father had liquidated what he could in order to give a large cash inheritance to the younger son, who promptly threw it all away. Everything that was left was the rightful inheritance of the elder son. As we observed very briefly in chapter 3, that son would not legally be able to take full and unrestricted ownership of the family estate until the death of the father. In other words, as long as the father lived, the elder son's own property rights were just usufructuary.

But in the elder son's case, that was a mere temporary formality. He *would* eventually inherit full title to everything that remained in the estate. That fact could not be changed now. When the inheritance was divided at the Prodigal Son's behest, legal arrangements would have been drawn up and executed to guarantee it. The elder son would automatically take sole possession when the father died. All questions about the long-term ownership of the family assets were already settled, legally binding, and absolutely irrevocable. There was no loophole by which the inheritance could be reapportioned. Everything on the property belonged to the elder brother by promise.

But for now, as long as the father was alive, he was still the family patriarch and head of the household. He technically held title to all the property for the time being, and therefore he had every prerogative to make use of the estate and all its assets any way he wished. In effect, what he did here was lay claim to everything he had promised to the elder son, and he told the younger son, "Use it however you like."

People listening to the parable would be perplexed at such an expression of grace. *How is that fair? How can the father reward the Prodigal so lavishly—in a way that almost seems insulting to the good-guy image of the elder son—in spite of the way the younger boy has behaved? How can this man permit the Prodigal Son to enjoy the same goods, benefits, and privileges as the son who stayed home?*

Had the Prodigal not returned, the elder son would have eventually worn that robe, or else the father himself would have used it at the elder son's wedding. That was the sort of occasion when such a robe should be brought out—the wedding of the firstborn son. Such a wedding was the single greatest event that would normally happen in any family. But now the robe was defiled with the younger brother's pig-stink.

> The father was granting the boy not only full forgiveness and full reconciliation but also the full privileges of a nobleman's son who has come of age and proved himself trustworthy.

The elder son should get the father's signet ring and the corresponding legal privilege of acting on his father's behalf. The elder son was the one who had stayed on the family property in the first place, and he should have sole usufructuary rights to it. After all, all that property was already his by a binding legal promise.

None of this made any sense, particularly in a culture where honor was so highly valued.

But the father acted quickly, without hesitation, and the firm and confident way he responded made his statement that much more emphatic. Consider once more in that light what a profound message this sent to the villagers who witnessed the scene: He put shoes on the Prodigal's feet as fast as possible, making a public, ceremonial statement that instantly eliminated any question about whether the boy's sonship was still intact. He called for the robe to be *brought* to the place where they were (v. 22), putting it on him before the boy could even go home and clean off the grime from his life of sin and the long journey home. He wanted the boy's rags covered as quickly as possible, before the Prodigal walked through the village under the disapproving gaze of so many people. He even covered the Prodigal in his own best garment, allowing that borrowed glory to serve as a shield against the shame the boy deserved. And he immediately gave him the ring, granting the boy an immense privilege he clearly was not worthy of enjoying.

Even more bizarre than that, the father treated the returning Prodigal like an honored prince. He ordered his servants to wait on his son as if the Prodigal were royalty: "You get the robe and put it on him; you put the sandals on his feet and the ring on his hand." The message was clear: the father was granting the boy not only full forgiveness and full reconciliation but also the full privileges of a nobleman's son who has come of age and proved himself trustworthy.

A Picture of God's Extravagant Grace

As Jesus described that scene, the crowd would be stunned with incredulity. Everything the father was doing for the son was exactly the opposite of what anyone thought he should do. It was contrary to that society's customs. It went against everything they knew about justice. And it flew in the face of common sense. Think of it: this boy instantly had all the same rights and privileges as his elder brother, who had never once overtly rebelled the way the Prodigal did. It was as if the journey to the far country had never happened. The father had absorbed blow after humiliating blow from this dishonorable son, and yet he was willing to set the past aside and freely endow this Prodigal Son with every conceivable privilege. There was no waiting period, no proving time, no hoops for the boy to jump through, and no readjustment phase. All the privileges were free and unrestricted. The boy was entering all at once into full-blown sonship at the highest level.

What was the message? We need to remind ourselves once again that this is a picture of God's lavish grace, which triumphs over every imaginable kind of sin. God saves sinners—including the very *worst* of sinners. And when He does, He instantly elevates the newly reborn sinner to a position of privilege and blessing that is exceedingly and abundantly beyond anything we could ever ask or think (cf. Ephesians 3:20).

> The scribes and Pharisees were so seriously wrong that the very religion they counted on to earn themselves eternal life would actually spell their destruction.

Again, while the grace and privilege extended to this son may seem exaggerated, it is no caricature. It is not really even extreme enough to serve as a proper illustration of the grace God actually and truly grants to repentant sinners. It's merely a scaled-back, toned-down, barely adequate figurative depiction of what authentic grace is like. Because mere human words and imagery are completely inadequate to illustrate the reality of God's mercy.

Yet this whole idea—that lavish love and extreme grace could be bestowed upon a penitent, trusting sinner—was absolutely bizarre in the legalistic minds of the scribes and Pharisees. They understood the concept of high privilege. They were convinced that legitimate privileges such as these could only be earned through a system of rigorous works and the strict accounting of personal merit. That's what their religion was all about.

But the scribes and Pharisees were so seriously wrong that the very religion they counted on to earn themselves eternal life would actually spell their destruction. That's why Jesus was calling them to confess their own need for divine grace and repent of their self-righteousness.

AN EXTRAORDINARY CELEBRATION

Having ceremonially crowned his repentant son with the highest honor and privilege, the Prodigal's father still was not finished. Next, he called for the party to end all parties: "Bring the fatted calf here and kill it, and let us eat and be merry; for this my son was dead and is alive again; he was lost and is found.' And they began to be merry" (Luke 15:23–24).

The fact that one man living with his elder son had a "fatted calf" on hand is one of the main signals Jesus gives that they were not merely well-to-do; they were extremely wealthy. They had a special calf, well fed and deliberately underexercised, in order to produce the most tender, tasty, prime meat. The Greek expression translated "fatted" literally means grain fed. So that calf would provide the choicest grain-fed veal. That's an expensive luxury even today. But in first-century culture, where any kind of meat was consumed only on special occasions and range-fed meat from full-grown cattle was an expensive commodity, no one but the wealthiest landowner would even think of feeding precious grain to an animal.

Such a calf would be fattened only for an extraordinary occasion, such as the wedding of a firstborn son or a once-in-a-lifetime banquet held to celebrate the arrival of an important dignitary. The animal would be carefully selected well in advance of the occasion, generously fed, diligently cared for, and kept penned up, apart from the herd. Timing the breeding process around the planned event was crucial, because calves obviously don't remain calves very long. Corn-fed veal is typically slaughtered when the calf is about five months old. To have an extra fatted calf on hand would be highly unusual (if not totally unheard of).

So it appears this father decided that the return of his wayward son was a more monumental reason for celebration than whatever event he was already planning. He could easily substitute some lesser fare and scale back the menu he was preparing for the other event. But *this* event, the sudden return of his long-lost son, called for the most massive of all celebrations—a megafeast. For that, he must kill the fatted calf.

> This father decided that the return of his wayward son was a more monumental reason for celebration than whatever event he was already planning.

By the way, the average five-month-old corn-fed veal calf weighs some five hundred pounds. It would be enough to feed hundreds of people. (The better cuts alone would easily provide more than enough for two hundred people, and since everything usable would go into some dish or another, a calf like this would provide massive amounts of food.) Preparations would take the rest of the day, and the festivities would continue deep into the night. It would not be unusual for a gala such as this to last three days or more. Everyone in the village would be invited.

This was undoubtedly the greatest event and the grandest celebration that had ever happened in that family. It was probably the biggest affair the village had ever seen. From the perspective of the father, that was fitting. No event could bring more joy to him than the return of his lost son. And here again we have a vivid picture of heaven's joy whenever one lost sinner repents.

The father's great joy is evident in his words: "For this my son was dead and is alive again; he was lost and is found" (Luke 15:24). Whether or not he had literally held the customary funeral service for his son when the boy fled into the far country, this father clearly reckoned the boy dead. He had a very frail hope but no real expectation that he would ever see the boy again. He had been living with that grief, in a constant state of bereavement, mourning the loss of a precious son, since the day the Prodigal walked away. He longed for the boy's return, pictured in his mind what it would be like to see him restored, and prayed for the opportunity to grant his forgiveness.

He had hardly dared to hope for such a day as this, but now it had finally arrived. The son who was dead was now "up and alive." (That's the literal meaning of the expression in verse 24.) The boy who was lost had at last been found. The father had the great joy he had long dreamed about, to hand the son his life back. The son now had a new status and a new attitude. Father and son were at last reconciled. For first time ever, the Prodigal had a real, vital relationship with a loving, forgiving father who gave him full rights to everything he possessed, and blessing upon blessing.

We could hardly blame the Prodigal Son for feeling like he had more reason to celebrate than anyone. He had entrusted his life to the father, and the father had absolutely amazed and overwhelmed him by entrusting his resources to him. The son was finally home, in the father's house, a true member of the family. He had every reason to remain faithful and devote the rest of his life to his father's honor.

THE CAUSE FOR THE CELEBRATION

Now, consider an important truth that is patently obvious but not expressly spelled out for us in Jesus' telling of the parable: this celebration was not about the son's behavior. Even his repentance—as wonderful as it was—did not merit this kind of extravagant honor.

What, exactly, was this party celebrating? A moment's thought will yield a clear answer because it is, after all, the whole theme of Luke 15. This was about the sheer joy of redemption.

In effect, then, the celebration was really in honor of the father's goodness to his undeserving son. The father is rejoicing not because the son has somehow managed to do something to earn his favor (the boy really *hadn't* done anything truly praiseworthy). But the father was rejoicing because he now had the long-awaited opportunity to forgive and restore the son who had so badly dishonored him and brought him so much grief.

> The celebration was really in honor of the father's goodness to his undeserving son.

In other words, the celebration here is for the father's sake, not the son's. The feast in effect honors the father. It was the father who gave this boy back his life and his privileges. It was the father who forgave him, restored him to sonship, gave him true liberty, and showered him with tokens of love. So this father, who apparently felt no shame, threw a party so that he could share the joy of his own kindness with everyone. That kind of joy is infectious, exhilarating, refreshing, and full of glory. It is a superbly suitable picture of heaven's joy.

I love the language at the end of verse 24, "They *began* to be merry" (emphasis added). This was only the start. And this is the picture of a party that never ends.

That's what heaven's joy is all about. It is the eternal celebration of the extravagant grace of a loving Father to penitent, believing, but altogether unworthy sinners. Heaven's joy doesn't *end* when a sinner comes home; that's only the beginning. Did you ever wonder what the saints will do in heaven? This is how we will spend eternity—in never-ending celebration of the joy of our heavenly Father.

A PICTURE OF HEAVEN'S JOY

While we are still considering the Prodigal's father, let's take note of some of the key lessons we can draw from Jesus' imagery. Remember that the father in the parable is a figure of Christ. He is the one who bears the sinner's reproach, invites repentant sinners to come to Him for rest, and embraces all who do come. He said, "The one who comes to Me I will by no means cast out" (John 6:37). There is an endless supply of mercy with Him. We can go boldly before Him and obtain mercy and grace to help in time of need (Hebrews 4:16). He replaces the rotten rags of our sin with the perfect robe of His own righteousness (Isaiah 61:10). He offers forgiveness, honor, authority, respect, responsibility, full access to all His riches, and the full right to pray in His name.

The father's eagerness to forgive reveals to us something about the divine perspective of redemption. Christ is not a reluctant Savior. God the Father himself is not the least bit reserved in extending mercy to penitent sinners. That's why 2 Corinthians 5:20 describes the Christian's role in bringing the gospel message to sinners as begging, pleading, urging people to be reconciled to God. We deliver that message, according to the apostle Paul, "on Christ's behalf"—as His ambassadors, speaking with His authority and declaring the message He Himself has issued for the benefit of all sinners everywhere.

Those facts, combined with the imagery in the parable of the prodigal son, picture God as almost impatient in His eagerness to forgive sinners. He runs to embrace. He showers the returning sinner with affection and kisses. He quickly calls for the robe,

> God's own joy is overflowing every time one sinner returns.

the ring, and the shoes. His justification is full and immediate—a finished reality, not merely an ethereal goal for the sinner to work for.

God's own joy is overflowing every time one sinner returns.

There's an effort afoot in these postmodern times, even within some quarters of the evangelical movement, to downplay the significance of personal redemption and the promise of heaven for individual believers. I keep hearing the suggestion that perhaps we have missed the real point of the gospel—that maybe it's not so much about the forgiveness of this or that person's sins, but it's all about bringing the kingdom of God to earth here and now. And so, we're told, Christians should be less concerned about their own personal redemption and more concerned about redeeming our culture or solving the large-scale dilemmas of our times, such as racial prejudice, global warming, poverty, the marginalization of disenfranchised people, or whatever worldwide crisis is slated to be the featured cause for the next Live Aid concert.

Earthly suffering is indeed an important issue for Christians. We need to care for the poor, minister to the sick and needy, comfort those who are sorrowing, and defend those who are genuinely oppressed.

But notice again that the divine joy Jesus talks about in Luke 15 is not unleashed because some great social problem in the world has finally been solved. Heaven's inhabitants are not waiting breathlessly to see whether the earth's environment can survive the effects of burning fossil fuels. The joy Jesus described is not currently suppressed under some divinely decreed moratorium until all the world's suffering can finally be eliminated. Nor is the start of the heavenly celebration on hold until a widespread revival at last breaks out somewhere.

All heaven rejoices "over *one sinner* who repents" (Luke 15:7; emphasis added). Since, there's every reason to believe individual sinners are being redeemed somewhere in the world all the time, day in and day out—it seems safe to assume that the party in heaven never stops. All heaven is filled with a consummate, undiluted, and unspeakable joy. Best of all, that joy is constant and never-ending.

That is why God also commands His people here on earth to "rejoice in the Lord always" (Philippians 4:4). "Rejoice evermore" (1 Thessalonians 5:16 KJV).

> To refuse to enter into heaven's joy is practically the most irrational and wicked sin imaginable.

In fact, to refuse to enter into heaven's joy is practically the most irrational and wicked sin imaginable. Why would anyone refuse to share this father's gladness and celebrate the redemption of so tragic a boy? Yet we are about to meet the character who embodies that very resentment: the elder brother.

A DIFFERENT KIND OF CONCLUSION

Here the parable takes another shocking turn. This beautiful story has spanned just a few brief verses so far, but it has featured several glorious and vitally important lessons about redemption, forgiveness, justification by faith, and God's own joy in the salvation of sinners. The parable appears to be heading toward a supremely happy ending.

But suddenly the whole character of the story changes. The elder son comes on the scene. The story suddenly plummets toward a completely different kind of conclusion. And in the end, it drives home an urgent and ominous message for Israel's self-righteous religious elite.

This is one of the most profound and truly pivotal moments in the earthly life and teaching of Christ.

PART 4

The Elder Brother

～

Now his older son was in the field. And as he came and drew near to the house, he heard music and dancing. So he called one of the servants and asked what these things meant. And he said to him, "Your brother has come, and because he has received him safe and sound, your father has killed the fatted calf." But he was angry and would not go in. Therefore his father came out and pleaded with him. So he answered and said to his father, "Lo, these many years I have been serving you; I never transgressed your commandment at any time; and yet you never gave me a young goat, that I might make merry with my friends. But as soon as this son of yours came, who has devoured your livelihood with harlots, you killed the fatted calf for him." And he said to him, "Son, you are always with me, and all that I have is yours. It was right that we should make merry and be glad, for your brother was dead and is alive again, and was lost and is found."

—Luke 15:25–32

NINE

His Resentment

He was angry and would not go in.

—Luke 15:28

SINNERS COME IN TWO BASIC VARIETIES. SOME ARE straightforward and intrepid in their evildoing, and they don't really care who sees what they do. Invariably, their besetting sin is pride—the kind of pride that is seen in an undue love for oneself and uncontrollable lusts for self-indulgent pleasures.

At the other end of the spectrum are secretive sinners, who prefer to sin when they think no one else is looking. They try to mask their more obvious sins in various ways—often with the pretense of religion. Their besetting sin is also pride, but it's the kind of pride that manifests itself in hypocrisy.

There are varying degrees and mixtures of those two types of sinners, of course, and the two obviously have a lot in common—like two brothers whose personalities make them seem very different, even though genetically they might be nearly identical.

Of the two types of sinners, the wanton sinner is much more likely than the sanctimonious sinner to face the reality of his own fallenness, repent, and seek salvation. His sin is already uncovered. It is undeniable. He *has* to face up to it. Not so with the Pharisee. He will try as long as possible to camouflage his immorality, deny his guilt, disavow his need for redemption, and declare his own righteousness.

That's why Jesus repeatedly said things like, "Those who are well have no need of a physician, but those who are sick" (Matthew 9:12).

In Jesus' parable, the Prodigal Son obviously represents open sinners—the rebels, the dissolute, the debauched, the deliberately immoral people who make no pretense of faith in God or love for Him. In other words, the character of the Prodigal is a symbol for those whom we encountered back in verse 1: "the tax collectors and the sinners"—society's outcasts. Such people start out by running as far away as possible from God. They have no innate love for Him. They desire no relationship with Him. They want nothing to do with His law or His authority. They have no interest in fulfilling someone else's expectations or demands—*especially* God's. They want no accountability to Him whatsoever. They don't even want to retain Him in their thoughts.

The apostle Paul gave this description of prodigal people in Romans 1:28–32:

> Even as they did not like to retain God in their knowledge, God gave them over to a debased mind, to do those things which are not fitting; being filled with all unrighteousness, sexual immorality, wickedness, covetousness, maliciousness; full of envy, murder, strife, deceit, evil-mindedness; they are whisperers, backbiters, haters of God, violent, proud, boasters, inventors of evil things, disobedient to parents, undiscerning, untrustworthy, unloving, unforgiving, unmerciful; who, knowing the righteous judgment of God, that those who practice such things are deserving of death, not only do the same but also approve of those who practice them.

In other words, prodigal sinners have no relationship to God whatsoever—not even in pretense. They don't love God, they don't care about Him, they give Him as little thought as possible, and they want nothing to do with the family of God.

Amazingly, Scripture repeatedly describes God's attitude toward these prodigal sinners by comparing it to the agony of rejected love (Ezekiel 33:11; Hosea 11:7–8; Matthew 23:37; Romans 10:21). With a profound expression of divine sorrow, God finally lets them go. That's what Romans 1:28 means when it says "God gave them over." He "gave them up to uncleanness" (v. 24). He "gave them up to vile passions" (v. 26). He let them go to pursue their open rebellion. Multitudes of sinners who are just like that—the vast majority of them, it seems—never do repent or return. But God's joy is effusive over those who do. And His mercy toward them is boundless.

As Jesus continues with His parable, it becomes obvious that the second (and opposite) kind of sinner is epitomized by the elder brother. This young man is an emblem of all the seemingly honorable, superficially moral, or outwardly religious sinners—people just like the scribes and Pharisees. Here is a sinner who thinks hypocrisy is as good as real righteousness. What he looks like on the outside cloaks a seething rebellion on the inside.

The elder son is the third major character in the parable, and as it turns out, he is the one who embodies the parable's main lesson. His most obvious characteristic is his resentment for his younger brother. But underneath that, and even more ominously, it is clear that he has been nurturing a quietly smoldering hatred for the father—for a long, long time, it appears. This secretly rebellious spirit has shaped and molded his character in a most disturbing way.

> The elder son is the third major character in the parable, and as it turns out, he is the one who embodies the parable's main lesson.

Luke 15:25–28 says, "Now his older son was in the field. And as he came and drew near to the house, he heard music and dancing. So he called one of the servants and asked what these things meant.

And he said to him, 'Your brother has come, and because he has received him safe and sound, your father has killed the fatted calf.' But he was angry and would not go in."

People often assume that the elder son represents a true believer, faithful all his life but suddenly caught off guard by his father's generosity to the wayward brother and therefore a little bit resentful. By that interpretation, the elder brother really needed nothing more than an attitude adjustment.

> The elder brother turns out to be just as lost and hopelessly enslaved to sin as his brother ever was. He just won't admit that—not to himself, or to anyone else.

That interpretation misses the whole point of the parable, though. The elder son has *never* truly been devoted to his father. He is by no means symbolic of the true believer. Instead, he depicts the religious hypocrite. He is the Pharisee figure in Jesus' story. He probably had the whole village sincerely believing that he was the "good" son—very respectful and faithful to his father. He stuck around the house. He pretended to be a loyal son. But in reality, he had no genuine respect for his father, no interest in what pleased his father, no love for the father's values, and no concern for his needy younger brother. That all becomes very clear as the story unfolds.

The elder brother turns out to be just as lost and hopelessly enslaved to sin as his brother ever was. He just won't admit that—not to himself or to anyone else.

RECAPPING THE STORY
FROM A PHARISEE'S POINT OF VIEW

Jesus was a master storyteller, and He knew exactly how to pull His audience into His stories. The Pharisees were about to become part of this tale in a most unexpected way. They had been following the narrative and making ethical judgments with every turn of the plot. But up to this point they were still listening from the perspective of onlookers. Until now, they had stood comfortably outside the story, passing judgment on the Prodigal, his father, and even Jesus. Pharisees always enjoy that kind of thing. Something about being shocked and outraged by the conduct of other people is just plain fun for any true Pharisee. So they were paying close attention to Jesus' story, even if only to be critical.

Then Jesus ingeniously turned the tables on them and put *them* under the microscope.

Imagine for a moment that you are one of the scribes or Pharisees— a legalist—listening as Jesus tells this story. In your assessment, practically everything the characters in this story have done up to this point has been permeated with shame. The Prodigal Son's escapades were scandalous. The father's rush to forgive was appalling. A huge banquet where all the villagers became participants in the merrymaking capped it all off with yet another disgraceful event—a veritable celebration of shame.

Along the way, you have been producing gasps, exclamations, and gestures in all the places where you felt you needed to make your disapproval known. When the son demanded his inheritance, you frowned deeply and shook your head. When the father gave him what he asked for, you muttered in protest. When the boy quickly squandered all his wealth, you exclaimed about the shame of it all. When he took a job tending pigs, you gasped in horror and wrung your hands. And so on. Certain aspects of the story have been mystifying to you, such as the Prodigal's repentance and his decision to come home. But then suddenly you were outraged again because of the father's unexpected clemency. Finally, the elaborate feast just left you shaking your head.

To your way of thinking, the father's determination to celebrate is in some ways the most troubling occurrence so far. It's something you could not possibly have foreseen, and you do not like the direction the story is headed at the moment.

Nevertheless, the story has drawn you in, because its major themes are the very things you care most about: honor and shame, earning approval versus deserving wrath, maintaining a proper appearance as contrasted with openly sinning, and being rewarded for doing well as opposed to being scorned for doing wrong. You have followed the story with the expectation that those who have acted so shamefully will somehow in the end reap the appropriate consequences.

In short, you are waiting for one of the characters to do something you perceive as right and honorable. The elder brother is your last, best hope. Here comes someone any Pharisee could identify with. You think to yourself, *Surely at last, this guy will set the story right.*

THE ELDER BROTHER TAKES CENTER STAGE

The Prodigal Son's brother had been out in the field that day. He was most likely overseeing a crew of servants who did the hard work while he told them what to do. Noblemen's sons of this stature did not normally need to do any dirty work for themselves. And since this particular young man was evidently as concerned as the Pharisees were about maintaining their honor, it seems unlikely that he would be doing anything beneath his dignity. But he was nevertheless "in the field" (Luke 15:25) and therefore completely oblivious to all that had happened in his father's life that day. That meant he was also unaware of the celebration that was already underway at his house, even though the whole rest of the village had been in a buzz about it for hours.

It appears that it was late in the evening, perhaps even dark already, when the elder brother showed up. We can deduce that from the noise of the celebration when he arrived. A party such as this would commence in a very imprecise way. (Life in that culture was not governed by the clock the way our events are today.) Before the workday was over, the announcement would go out—in this case, no doubt, as a general invitation to everyone in the village and its vicinity: "Come! We are killing the fatted calf. The nobleman's son has come home, and they are having a feast." People would begin to arrive in the late evening, after the workday was finished and they had time to dress for the party. The real festivities would begin around sundown, and as more and more people arrived, the celebration would become louder and livelier. Singing and celebrating continued well into the night as the ebb and flow of this wonderful celebration took place.

The party was already full blown when the elder son arrived and discovered to his complete surprise what was happening. These details are significant on several counts. First of all, it is yet more evidence that this family's estate was enormous and the family lands were vast. The field where the elder brother was working must have been someplace remote in order for him not to catch wind of the goings-on in the village and at the house all day—especially once the musicians, dancers, and hundreds of guests began arriving. Furthermore, the lateness of his arrival indicates that he had come from a long way off.

More significant, however, is the fact that he walked into this celebration completely oblivious to the fact that any such event had been planned. Here was the biggest event the village had ever seen—the greatest celebration his family had ever hosted—and he knew nothing about it.

It is a striking fact that neither the father nor anyone else had told the elder son about his brother's return. In all the excitement,

> It is a striking fact that neither the father nor anyone else had told the elder son about his brother's return.

no messenger had been sent to bring him the glad tidings, and (even more telling) he had not even been asked to assist with preparations for the celebration. That is extremely surprising because with so much to coordinate and so many tasks and people requiring oversight, the help of someone with the clout of a nobleman's firstborn son would certainly be a great benefit. In fact, the responsibility for setting up and overseeing the arrangements for an event like this in that culture would normally fall on the shoulders of the eldest son. Party planning was hardly a patriarchal duty.

In this case, however, before the elder boy even came into the picture, all the preparations were complete, the entire village had been summoned, musicians and dancers were already leading the festivities, and the party was well and truly under way. Why was he not told before this?

There's only one reasonable explanation. This son had no better relationship with his father than the Prodigal did when he first left home. The father surely knew that—even if no one else did. Sure, the elder brother was still living at home. An onlooker from outside the family might not notice any obvious tension between the father and his firstborn. But all his supposed faithfulness and compliance with the father's will was just a sham. It was nothing more than *his* way of getting what he wanted—approval, affirmation, wealth, land, and prestige in the community. In reality, this boy was every bit as estranged from the father as his openly rebellious younger brother had ever been.

The elder brother had already given clear evidence of that at the beginning of the story when he did nothing to dissuade his brother from taking his portion of the inheritance and leaving home. If he had been the least bit interested in his father's honor, he ought to have done something to defend it. Instead, he likewise took his part of the inheritance gladly, no doubt pleased to benefit so richly from the younger boy's open rebellion while maintaining the thin veneer of his own respectability. The elder son was actually guilty of a more passive—but equally sinister—form of rebellion, and his actions here prove it. He had no relationship with anyone in the family— not the father, and certainly not his younger brother.

The fact that he was not quickly summoned as soon as the Prodigal arrived seems to be clear evidence that at least the father could see what was really in the elder brother's heart. The father knew the real truth about his first-born son, even if it wasn't obvious to everyone else.

> The elder son was actually guilty of a more passive—but equally sinister— form of rebellion, and his actions here prove it.

That's why the celebration began without him. The father probably anticipated how the elder brother would react to his brother's home-coming, and therefore he deliberately did not bring him into the process early. He didn't need this young man's sour, sulking attitude to be a wet blanket on such a festive occasion. Besides, the boy's passive-aggressive antagonism would have been no help at all—in fact, it would have been a serious impediment during the preparatory stages of putting on a great feast like this. So the father simply let the elder son remain in the field while he himself organized the celebration, invited the guests, began the party, and acted as sole host.

A HOMECOMING OF A DIFFERENT SORT

Just as the younger son's fleeing to the far country serves to show how poorly he regarded his father, so this one's being out in the field is a fitting metaphor for where he stood in terms of his own family. Both sons were far away from the father. In the end they both came home—but with totally different attitudes and to very different receptions.

As the elder son approached the house, "he heard music and dancing" (v. 25). This was typical at wedding feasts and other festive occasions. It was a celebratory style of music, normally led by professional instrumentalists and singers who were hired to maximize the joyfulness of the atmosphere. Guests' voices would join in the singing, and a group of men would typically form a circle and dance, while women and children stood on the outer perimeter clapping rhythmically and singing along. It was deliberately loud and raucous, and with a party this size, the elder son probably began to hear it while he was still more than half a mile away.

The smell of roasted meat would also permeate the air. The fattened calf had been killed. Typically, the meat would be carved into large roasts, which would be slow-cooked in wood-burning bread ovens. Large slabs of the veal roasts would be cooked sequentially so that while people who arrived early were eating, meat was continually being cooked for those who would come later. The serving continued for hours in an endless buffet. The aroma from that much meat cooking in fruitwood ovens would fill the atmosphere with a delightful scent that would likewise reach a fair distance.

The elder son, returning from the field without a clue what any of this signified, would easily detect all the signs of a great celebration in the air. He was surprised and understandably curious. *What could this possibly mean?*

Of course there was no reason whatsoever for him to make any negative assumptions. Anyone coming upon a scene like this *ought* to meet it with the highest expectations and an eager heart. All the music and dancing made it perfectly obvious, after all, that he was walking into a celebration, not a funeral. He ought to have been excited to learn what spectacularly good news could possibly have unleashed an unplanned celebration of this magnitude. You would think he would run to the noise and see for himself.

But not so. This young man was clearly in a glass-half-empty kind of mood. He was suspicious. (Legalists are almost always suspicious, particularly when they encounter joyful people.) He was stunned, confused, and clearly less than pleased to see such a party in full swing at his home but without his knowledge. After all, when he went out to the field that morning, it was a day like any other day. He had now come home at a late hour, and with no warning, he arrived to find the biggest celebration he had ever witnessed, already underway, and under his own roof.

> The elder brother's surprise is perfectly understandable; his extreme indignation is not so easily excused.

The elder brother's surprise is perfectly understandable; his extreme indignation is not so easily excused. His reaction suggests that he assumed from the get-go that whatever news had provoked such delirious joy on the part of his father was going to be something he would resent. So "he called one of the servants and asked what these things meant" (v. 26).

A Boycott Only a Pharisee Could Appreciate

If this son's heart were right—if he had even an ounce of genuine love or authentic concern for anyone in his family besides himself— the text would say, "He ran to the house to see what all the joy was about." In fact, if his heart had not been completely devoid of all natural filial affection, he would have run directly to his father, embraced him, and asked, "What glorious news are we celebrating? What's going on?" Then his father would have said, "Your brother's home," and they would have embraced and rejoiced together with tears.

The elder son must have known very well how much his father loved the younger brother. Anyone could easily see what a grief the man suffered when the boy rebelled and what an ache he had carried in his heart every single day since the Prodigal ran away. If the stay-at-home son had truly loved his dad, whatever made the father rejoice should have been an occasion for him to rejoice as well—*especially* something this near and dear to the father's heart.

But the elder brother did not respond that way. He remained outside, slowing to a halt before he reached the house, deliberately keeping his distance from the celebration. He demanded to know what was going on before he would even think of joining the festivities. Verse 26 says, "He called one of the servants and asked what these things meant."

The Greek word translated "servant" in that verse signifies a young, preadolescent boy. All the adult servants were inside, of course, taking care of guests. But household servants living on a large estate such as this would naturally have their own families. Some of them were young children. They were themselves called "servants" by virtue of the fact that they were born into servants' families. They might even occasionally run errands at the behest of the master, but they were still too young to be of much help during a gala such as this. So they would play together on the outer fringes of the celebration.

A huge event like this with so much food and the opportunity to stay up late into the night was obviously a joyous occasion for them too. The children would have their own little party outside, and in that way even the servants' children became participants in the joy of this wonderful celebration.

That was apparently the first group the elder brother met as he came in the direction of the house. Of course, he was a person of the highest rank in the household, so he was not someone the servant children would talk to casually. They even may have lowered their animated chatter to a whisper as he approached. But he summoned one of them over and asked what was going on. Actually, the language Jesus employed suggests that he *demanded* an explanation, not from his own father, but from someone who would be totally intimidated by him. The verb tense in verse 26 is imperfect, implying repeated action: "He *kept* inquiring." This suggests that he inundated the boy with a barrage of questions: *What is going on? How is it that I didn't know about this? Why wasn't I even consulted?*

The servant boy's answer implies that he expected the elder brother to welcome the good news: "Your brother has come, and because he has received him safe and sound, your father has killed the fatted calf" (v. 27). The Greek expression translated "safe and sound" in the English version is the same root from which our word *hygiene* is derived. It speaks of wholeness, cleansing, and health. The servant boy was not merely announcing that the Prodigal Son was finally home from the far country, but also that he was dramatically changed for the better. More important, the father had *received* him. Their relationship was restored. That's what this party was all about. The fatted calf that was being prepared for some other celebration had been slaughtered for this one instead. The servant boy's brief synopsis summed up the entire day's events in remarkably few words. It told the elder brother everything he needed to know.

But the elder brother was by no means pleased to hear the news. Given the cultural context, the seriousness of the younger boy's sin, and the fact that the elder brother had not yet seen the Prodigal or heard any expression of repentance from his own lips, we might not expect him to rise instantly to the same full height of joy his father had. But if this son felt any genuine love for his father at all, he would not have reacted to his brother's return as if it were *bad* news. At the very least, he ought to have been filled with some sense of relief to know that his brother was safely at home. He had witnessed the Prodigal's rebellion. He knew very well what kind of wicked, self-destructive attitude the boy left home with. Wouldn't it seem reasonable that he should be glad to learn that the boy was alive—and curious to see for himself how his younger brother might have changed?

But he was neither of those things. Instead, his immediate response was extreme anger. He refused to go in.

THE TRUE HEART OF THE ELDER SON REVEALED

Don't miss the real reason for the elder brother's intense displeasure. As we will see in the chapter that follows, all this pouting fury was not so much aimed at the Prodigal Son. Instead, it was focused directly against the father. This firstborn son clearly had no affection for his younger brother, but the father was the one whom he most resented.

> This firstborn son clearly had no affection for his younger brother, but the father was the one whom he most resented.

He could tell from the servant's report that his father had made peace with the Prodigal. The father had not only "received him safe and sound," but he had "killed the fatted calf, too" (v. 27). The meaning of such a gesture was clear. The father had already fully forgiven the wayward boy, and their reconciliation was complete.

It wasn't even as if the miscreant showed up looking for help and the tenderhearted father was now thinking about a suitable punishment for him. Apparently, the father wasn't requiring the Prodigal to make any kind of restitution or devising a scheme for him to earn his reconciliation. That would not be necessary now. It was obvious to all that the father had already received his son in peace, fully forgiven him, and now was throwing this lavish block party to honor rather than shame the boy.

Worst of all, in order to do it, the father was spending resources that would rightfully belong to the elder brother as soon as the father died—in effect, diminishing the value of the "faithful" son's inheritance.

Understand: this elder son didn't care at all about the father's joy. He wasn't interested in joining the celebration. All he cared about were his own rights and possessions. The elder brother was every bit as self-seeking and devoid of true appreciation for the father as the Prodigal Son was at the beginning of the parable.

But for the first time in the story, the Pharisees were saying to themselves, *Yes! That is* exactly *the right attitude! That is precisely what any self-respecting person ought to feel. He is right to be outraged. We are outraged. This whole story has described one atrocity after another, and it's about time someone in the story spoke up and said so.*

This is an exact mirror of the real-life situation we saw at the very beginning of Luke 15: "All the tax collectors and the sinners drew near to Him to hear [Jesus]. And the Pharisees and scribes complained, saying, "This Man receives sinners and eats with them" (vv. 1–2). The scribes and Pharisees remained outside the celebration. They resented it. They were outraged by it. It was a scandal and an affront to their dignity.

The elder son is a perfect emblem for the Pharisees. He had no appreciation for grace because he thought he didn't need it. As we shall soon observe, he figured he had *earned* his father's full approval without recourse to any special grace or mercy. If he didn't need grace and had never even thought to ask for any, he didn't see why grace should be offered to anyone else.

The truth is, he didn't really even believe in grace. He might have given lip service to the word. He probably talked about God's mercy and forgiveness as though he really believed in those virtues. But in reality, he thought of such things as favors to be earned rather than wholly gracious blessings that can only be granted freely. He had no concept of unmerited favor. The very idea of free forgiveness was repugnant to him.

Naturally, with such a view of grace, the father's forgiveness toward the Prodigal Son seemed like a deliberate slight to the elder brother. The wayward son was receiving honors the elder, more faithful boy had never once been offered. It was an insult to him. He was stunned. He was outraged. He was confused. But mostly, he was resentful.

On a completely human level, such a response might seem understandable. But it was in fact the ultimate proof that this elder son had no true love for his father. If he really wanted to honor his father, here was the perfect opportunity. If he weren't so consumed with himself, his own prestige, his own property, and his own selfish agenda, he might have seen that. But the truth is, this son was secretly much *more* of a rebel than the Prodigal had ever been. He wasn't as obvious in showing his contempt for the father as the Prodigal had once been, but he privately nurtured the same wicked heart of rebellion, the same lusts, and the same selfish attitude. He tried hard to keep his sour spirit carefully covered up, but that only added hypocrisy to the list of evils he had committed against his father. His steadfast refusal to see his father's point of view and repent of his self-centeredness is what made his brand of rebellion even worse than his brother's.

> The truth is, this son was secretly much *more* of a rebel than the Prodigal had ever been.

That was precisely the spiritual state of the scribes and Pharisees who criticized Jesus for consorting with sinners. It was exactly the kind of self-obsession and egocentric religious fervor their system fostered. Jesus likened them to fancy burial vaults—bright and shiny on the outside but full of death and decay on the inside (Matthew 23:27). They were religious hypocrites who stayed near the house of God for the sake of their own public image. But they secretly enjoyed all the same evil things as an unbeliever.

Even all the Pharisees' religious activity was really only about their own self-promotion. They may have truly thought they were earning the good will of God. But the truth is that they were completely alienated from God. They had no sincere desire to honor Him. They had no vital interest in heaven's joy—in fact, they could not even tolerate that joy because it was joy over the repentance of sinners, and they refused to confess their own need for repentance. So they openly spurned the joy, and they deeply resented those who did repent.

As Jesus continued with the parable and the Pharisees began to recognize themselves in the elder brother, their murmured expressions of displeasure must have begun to rise in a deafening crescendo. The lesson the Lord had been laying the groundwork for from the start of the parable was about to become very, very clear—and by now they might even see it coming.

TEN

His True Character

Lo, these many years I have been serving you; I never transgressed your commandment at any time; and yet you never gave me a young goat, that I might make merry with my friends.

—Luke 15:29

THOSE FAMILIAR WITH JESUS' PARABLES WILL BE AWARE that the plot, characters, and main lesson of the Prodigal Son's story bear a number of intriguing similarities to a much shorter parable recorded in Matthew 21. That parable was also about two sons. Jesus told it at the height of one of His most dramatic face-to-face encounters with Israel's religious elite.

The Matthew 21 parable is especially remarkable for its blunt antagonism, aimed squarely at the chief priests and elders—the highest ranking religious leaders in all Israel at the time. Jesus told it on *their* turf (or so they supposed)—in the temple grounds at Jerusalem. They were the ones who had initiated this hostile encounter in order to confront *Him*. But He turned the situation around and put them on the spot instead. Jesus used the parable of the prodigal son to illustrate and unmask the Pharisees' hypocrisy. Then He forced them to acknowledge with their own lips that it is better for an openly sinful person to repent than for someone who denies being a sinner to shield his sin behind a facade of respectable hypocrisy.

Those priestly dignitaries were (to say the least) unaccustomed to being cross-examined like that. But Jesus still wasn't finished. He followed up the parable with a curt denunciation of their whole approach to religion. Here, briefly, is what happened.

> Jesus used the parable of the prodigal son to illustrate and unmask the Pharisees' hypocrisy.

It was late in Jesus' earthly ministry. One day before this, He had cleansed the temple for the second and final time in His three years (Matthew 21:12–14; cf. John 2:13–18), driving out the hucksters and money changers who were making an illicit profit off worshipers, and who gave the temple a carnival atmosphere. So this group of eminent temple authorities approached Him publicly, challenging him, "By what authority are You doing these things? And who gave You this authority?" (Matthew 21:23). At last, they would force Jesus to state plainly whose authority was behind His teaching.

Of course, they knew Jesus' answer to their question perfectly well by then. It appears they were looking for a way to charge Him with blasphemy. And if they couldn't do that, perhaps they could find a way to embarrass Him. So they had decided on a question they were sure would back Him into a corner. If he claimed to be teaching with the authority of God, they would charge Him with blasphemy. But if he claimed any lesser authority, they could trump Him with an appeal to their tradition.

Jesus agreed to answer their question—but only if they would first answer a similar question He had for them. His question was about the authority behind John's baptism: "Where was it from? From heaven or from men?" (Matthew 21:25).

Now He had *them* cornered. Since John the Baptist had been openly hostile to the institutionalized hypocrisy of Israel's religious leaders (Matthew 3:7–11), his immense popularity among the common people was a serious problem for them. Most people in Israel firmly believed John to be a great prophet, so if the temple leaders openly questioned John's authority, they could expect a serious backlash. But if they affirmed John's authority, they would be condemned for not following him.

John the Baptist had been beheaded by Herod at least a year before this (Matthew 14:1–11). That solved one problem for the Jewish leaders by silencing someone whom they regarded as a gadfly and fanatic. But it also made John a martyr, dramatically elevating his popularity throughout all of Israel. So these religious leaders desperately needed to pretend they were neutral about John the Baptist. Although they actually opposed everything he stood for, they more or less tried to keep quiet about him.

Jesus' question put pressure right on their sore spot. Either way they answered, they would be the subject of scorn from the people. Therefore they simply refused to answer and pretended ignorance instead: "We do not know" (Matthew 21:27).

Jesus likewise declined to answer their question about His authority. But now He had *another* question for them. He put it to them by giving them the parable of the two sons:

"A man had two sons, and he came to the first and said, 'Son, go, work today in my vineyard.' He answered and said, 'I will not,' but afterward he regretted it and went. Then he came to the second and said likewise. And he answered and said, 'I go, sir,' but he did not go. Which of the two did the will of his father?" They said to Him, "The first." Jesus said to them, "Assuredly, I say to you that tax collectors and harlots enter the kingdom of God before you." (vv. 28–31)

That is extremely harsh language, with an unusually sharp edge. Don't overlook the biting severity of Jesus' tone when you read it. Most people both then and now would be completely put off by the sheer, unqualified bluntness of Jesus' language—as well as His harsh attitude toward the religious elite. But the circumstances called for just such a shrill alarm.

Notice, too, that the symbolism of the two sons in that parable is crystal clear from its own context. The son who at first rebelled and then relented represents the "tax collectors and harlots" who came to Jesus for mercy and forgiveness. The son who said he would obey but didn't is a symbol of the religious elite—who made every pretense of faithfulness and obedience but were in fact the worst kind of unbelieving rebels.

The close parallels between that parable and the parable of the prodigal son are too obvious to miss. The symbolism of the two sons is exactly the same in both parables. In fact, the Matthew 21 story is virtually the same plot as the parable of the prodigal son, minus all the coloring and rich details of the story line. Jesus is making essentially the same point. He is showing the absolute folly of thinking hypocrites like the scribes and Pharisees deserved God's approval.

> The parable comes down to this: it is a very serious and urgent wake-up call for scribes, Pharisees, chief priests, and any other religious person who is hypocritical and self-righteous.

In the end, He said, tax collectors and prostitutes who repent will enter the kingdom of heaven, but the most diligently religious Pharisees will not—unless they likewise repent and acknowledge their total dependence on divine grace and God's righteousness rather than their own good works and self-righteousness.

That, as we have seen, is ultimately the message of the parable of the prodigal son as well. At the end of all the colorful details, the shocking plot twists, the human-interest features, and even the poignancy of the Prodigal Son's redemption, the parable comes down to this: it is a very serious and urgent wake-up call for scribes, Pharisees, chief priests, and any other religious person who is hypocritical and self-righteous.

What are the characteristics of such people? Several of them are clearly evident in the Prodigal Son's elder brother as he angrily responds to his father.

HIS ANIMOSITY OVER THE CELEBRATION

Let's pick up the scene right where we left off at the end of the previous chapter. The elder brother, returning home late, arrives to find a celebration the likes of which he has never seen. He has just learned from a servant boy that his younger brother has come home, that the father has already forgiven the Prodigal and received him with joy, and that he has killed the fatted calf for a massive feast to celebrate the boy's redemption. As we saw in the previous chapter, the elder brother asked for and received no elaboration on any of those facts. He wasn't seeking further information. He had already heard enough. "He was angry and would not go in" (Luke 15:28).

His anger here gives us a pretty good insight into his real character. It reveals what he had been bottling up inside all along. This son may have worked hard to keep a respectable facade, but on the inside, he was filled with bitterness that had already reached the boiling point and was ready at the slightest provocation to explode into absolute fury.

What, really, did the elder son have to be indignant about? His father's joy over the younger boy's repentance and return was no insult to him. It was not as if the father now despised his own firstborn son just because he had forgiven the younger son. By expressing his great love for the Prodigal and his joy over the boy's return, the father was not saying anything negative about the older boy. Parental love isn't parceled out in finite amounts, so that whatever special love he showed to one son automatically diminished his feelings for the other. He certainly ought to be able to rejoice over a lost son's return without it being perceived as a slight by the son who had not run away.

But as we saw in the previous chapter, there is plenty of clear evidence in the narrative to suggest that this son was just as rebellious in his own way as the Prodigal Son had been at the height of his folly. His behavior was different from his brother's, but his heart was full of the same lusts and desires. We've already seen one clear expression of this son's rebelliousness in his hesitation and suspicion when he first arrived and discovered the celebration. And now his secret spirit of defiance is confirmed beyond all doubt by his petulant refusal to take part in his father's great joy.

By now the Pharisees were probably tuned in to the reality that, in Jesus' imagery, the elder brother was a mirror in which they could see themselves. If they hadn't picked up on it already, the phrase "He was angry and would not go in" certainly should have clued them in.

> By now the Pharisees were probably tuned in to the reality that in Jesus' imagery, the elder brother was a mirror in which they could see themselves.

Remember, what set off this string of parables in the first place was the complaint of the scribes and Pharisees that Jesus "receives sinners and eats with them." Everything from that statement (v. 2) until "he . . . would not go in" (v. 28) has built relentlessly to this point, and the sinfulness of the Pharisees' attitude was about to be unmasked.

Joy permeates the rest of Luke 15. The shepherd who found his sheep was so glad that he had a formal celebration for all his "friends and neighbors" (v. 6). The woman who searched for the lost coin until she found it could not contain her joy, so she likewise called her "friends and neighbors" together for a formal celebration (v. 9). Now the Prodigal Son's grateful father was so overwhelmed with joy to get his son back that he threw the grandest celebration ever and invited the entire town. So there is no question that the insuppressible joy of finding that which was lost is the recurring theme that dominates this whole chapter.

In all three parables, only one person refused the invitation to rejoice: this angry elder brother. His sullenness is all the more remarkable for the way it stands out starkly against the backdrop of so much joy.

The point *should* have been crystal clear: since these three parables were lessons about God's own delight in the salvation of sinners, and since the celebrations were emblematic of the feast of the redeemed who participate in heaven's joy—then the person who angrily stands outside the banquet and refuses to go in must face the reality he has excluded himself from the kingdom of God alto-

> The person who angrily stands outside the banquet and refuses to go in must face the reality he has excluded himself from the kingdom of God altogether.

gether. In other words, when the firstborn son crossed his arms, stood his ground, and refused to enter his father's celebration, that was an illustration of the very thing Jesus Himself made explicit at the end of the parable of the two sons in Matthew 21, when He turned to the religious leaders and said: "Assuredly, I say to you that tax collectors and harlots enter the kingdom of God before you" (Matthew 21:31).

The Prodigal's brother gives us a vivid depiction of how the Pharisees saw things. He illustrates why they were so haughty and hateful in their dealings with others. They disdained the idea that divine grace was sufficient to save sinners. They resented the mercy of immediate forgiveness. They scoffed at Jesus' teaching that sinners could be justified by faith and instantly reconciled with the heavenly Father.

Most of the Pharisees had been laboring their entire lives to be respectable and to gain God's favor. And yet some of the most debauched sinners in that culture (tax collectors, prostitutes, and demon-possessed people) had found instant forgiveness and full fellowship with Christ. He typically forgave them at the very instant they began to express their repentance. But the Pharisees weren't even asked to oversee preparations for the celebratory feast. It wasn't fair. It wasn't equitable. This was not the kind of Messiah they bargained for.

> The Pharisees' chief error lay in their belief that they *did* deserve God's favor.

Now, let's acknowledge the one kernel of truth in the Pharisees' perspective. *Of course* sinners don't deserve forgiveness and eternal life. The Prodigal Son did not deserve all the favor his father showed him. That was absolutely true, and not one forgiven sinner or restored Prodigal Son would ever claim otherwise.

But the Pharisees' chief error lay in their belief that they *did* deserve God's favor.

The elder brother was about to give voice to that very sentiment, and any Pharisee willing to be honest with himself would have to acknowledge complete sympathy with this proud perspective:

> Lo, these many years I have been serving you; I never transgressed your commandment at any time; and yet you never gave me a young goat, that I might make merry with my friends. But as soon as this son of yours came, who has devoured your livelihood with harlots, you killed the fatted calf for him. (Luke 15:29–30)

We'll look more closely at that little soliloquy before this chapter ends, but for now, consider the single most glaring problem with the elder son's perspective: by despising the father's grace, he was condemning himself. Whether he was willing to admit it or not, the elder brother needed the father's forgiveness and mercy as much as the Prodigal did. Instead of resenting the father's kindness to his brother, this son should have been the most eager participant in the celebration because he, too, was in desperate need of that kind of mercy. If he had simply had an honest understanding of the wickedness of his own heart, he would have seized on the father's mercy as the greatest reason of all to rejoice.

The very same truths govern the spiritual realm. Apart from God's grace, no one has power to do anything *but* sin. So those who scorn the concept of amazing grace only condemn themselves. Their works may appear good on a superficial level. They may be very impressive from a merely human perspective.

But Scripture is clear: all human works, religious deeds, and acts of righteousness done with the notion of gaining God's approval are nothing but filthy rags in His estimation (Isaiah 64:6). They are tainted by impure motives. They are done with a desire for self-aggrandizement rather than for God's glory. They therefore feed sinful pride and breed gross hypocrisy. Graceless works of religion are imperfect by every measure, and therefore they are utterly abominable to God, who can tolerate no standard shy of His own absolute perfection.

That means grace is the *only* hope for any sinner. That's what this parable is about, and that is what the forgiveness of the Prodigal Son symbolizes. Those who repent and turn to Christ are fully forgiven and immediately covered with the garment of His own perfect righteousness. Thus they meet the impossible standard God requires—not through any doing of their own but through what Christ does on their behalf. That is how God justifies the ungodly (Romans 3:26).

And that is why the same haughty, angry attitude of the Pharisees that caused them to resent Christ's grace toward sinners was the very thing that sealed their own destruction.

HIS ENMITY AGAINST HIS FATHER

The father and his firstborn son in this parable are a study in contrasts. The father is kind and merciful, and he rejoices when his younger son repents. The elder brother was self-centered and cruelhearted, and he actually became angry over the father's kindness to his needy brother. It is a sorry display of childish exasperation, worthy of a swift rebuke from the father.

But the father made overtures every bit as tenderhearted and gracious to the elder son as the mercy he had shown to the

> The father was every bit as tenderhearted and gracious to the elder son as he had been to the Prodigal.

Prodigal. When word somehow came to him that his firstborn son was standing outside, refusing to come in, the father realized, of course, that this was an expression of angry rebellion on the elder son's part. Having endured the grief of the Prodigal's rebellion and just barely begun to taste the joy of his return and repentance, the father now had to contend with a second defiant son.

The rebellion long suppressed underneath the elder son's hypocrisy had now broken into the open. The father no doubt knew all along about the cursed enmity hidden away in his son's heart. (It would be well-nigh impossible for a son to keep that level of disaffection a total secret from the father.) But his contempt for the father had now broken to the surface as full-blown insolence.

Still, rather than scolding this son (or worse), the father dealt gently with him: "[He] came out and pleaded with him" (Luke 15:28). He actually walked away from the celebration and went outside, where the elder son was pouting. It is hard to conceive of anything else that might have caused the father to leave such a joyful occasion voluntarily in order to subject himself to a grief of this magnitude. But he was a gracious man, and he dearly loved both sons. So he began to entreat the elder son—pleading with him to set aside his bitterness, come inside, and join in the celebration.

Here is yet another picture of God—in Christ—as the one who makes the first proposal of peace to the sinner. He is (as always) the seeker and the initiator. Although in that culture the father still had every right to command his son, and the son had a duty to obey, this father wasn't looking for grudging compliance. He had already seen enough of that from this son. Therefore instead of commanding his firstborn son, he pleaded with him passionately.

> Here is yet another picture of God—in Christ— as the one who makes the first overture of peace to the sinner.

That, by the way, would have been nearly as much of a surprise to Jesus' audience as the tenderness the father showed earlier to the Prodigal. Fathers in that culture did not typically plead. They didn't have to; they wielded authority. And in a case like this, where the father was in effect being personally insulted by his own firstborn son's refusal to come to a celebratory banquet in his own house—no one in that society would have thought anything about it if the father had taken the boy inside and given him a public beating for his insolence. At the very least, he might have locked the son in a room somewhere until he could be properly dealt with.

Instead, the insulted father left his own celebration in order to beg the elder boy to relent of his despicable attitude. With nothing but mercy, he reached out to the boy the same way he had reached out to the returning Prodigal Son.

But this son's response was markedly different, and it further reveals how deep-rooted his resentment toward the father was. Fed up and angry, he tore the veil off his own hypocrisy and unloaded his bitterness with language and a tone that was clearly meant to be insulting. He was clearly enraged now, and he didn't care who knew it. Look at verses 29–30 again, this time from the New American Standard Bible:

> But he answered and said to his father, "Look! For so many years I have been serving you and I have never neglected a command of yours; and yet you have never given me a young goat, so that I might celebrate with my friends; but when this son of yours came, who has devoured your wealth with prostitutes, you killed the fattened calf for him.

With the very first word, "Look!" the deep enmity and disrespect toward his father this boy had tried all his life to conceal from public view suddenly erupted. Then, as today, for a son to address his father that way was a sign of utter contempt, and the viciousness in his tone is impossible to conceal, even in the printed version: "Look! For *so many years* I have been serving you" (empahsis added).

Even when the Prodigal was still in the far country, when he first began imagining how he would come back and ask to be made a servant, he planned and rehearsed how to address his dad with the utmost respect and affection as "Father." In fact, the opening words of the two sons' statements side by side make a striking contrast. The rebel speaks with humility and a high regard for his father: "Father, I have sinned . . ." (v. 18). The supposedly good, respectful son speaks with sheer arrogance and disrespect: "Look! For so many years I have been serving you" (v. 29).

The Greek text is even more revealing. The elder brother uses the word *doulos* to describe his role. Literally, it means, "For

176

all these years I have been your *slave*." That is a typical legalistic mentality. He was admitting that everything he had ever done for his father was done under a sense of compulsion, not gladly. His service to the father had been a drudgery equivalent to slavery in his own mind. His life at home was anything but a delight as far as he was concerned. He had no joy of his own and therefore was not the least bit interested in participating in the father's joy.

Why, then, did the elder brother remain at the task all those years? If his service to the father was such an odious thing to him, why did he not simply leave home the way the younger son did? The answer is simple if you think about it. He was the firstborn. He stood to inherit a double portion of the father's legacy, including the best and largest part of the land. He wasn't going to forfeit that for a cash payout the way his foolish brother did. But his attitude was the same as the Prodigal's had been at the start—perhaps even uglier. He, too, was basically wishing his father would die so that he could get on with his life.

> The firstborn son was in the very same place the younger son had started out. He wanted what he considered rightfully his, on his own terms, so that he could live however he pleased.

In the end, the firstborn son was in the very same place the younger son had started out. He wanted what he considered rightfully his, on his own terms, so that he could live however he pleased. He just had a different way of getting to that long-term goal. He lacked the boldness of his younger brother. He didn't have the moxie to run away. It was much easier for him just to wait until the father died, and then he would have what he wanted.

HIS AUDACITY IN DESCRIBING HIMSELF

The elder son's self-assessment is one of the most telling aspects of his whole rant. Listen as he expresses the typical hyperinflated self-image of a religious hypocrite: "I never transgressed your commandment at any time" (v. 29). He sounds like the rich young ruler who listened to Jesus' summary of the Ten Commandments and then blithely replied, "All these things I have kept from my youth. What do I still lack?" (Matthew 19:20).

What is it about hypocrisy that feeds pride? You might think someone who is a hypocrite could manage a modicum of humility to balance things out. After all, he of all people knows that what he pretends to be does not match the reality of who he really is. Why are people like that invariably proud as well?

The obvious answer is that they are as good at lying to themselves as they are at fooling others. They are therefore hopelessly self-deceived. Because the hypocrite *pretends* to be good, he is under the illusion that he has actually *done* good—and therefore he thinks he *is* good. Having done all his "good works" just to benefit himself, he naturally becomes self-satisfied. He buries the truth of who he is as deep inside as he can, smothers his conscience, and therefore has no difficulty maintaining the illusion in his own mind that he has never ever neglected a single command.

It seems we often hear from people like that nowadays. In this no-fault age where seared consciences are mass produced by public education, we have already seen two or three generations come to adulthood having been thoroughly indoctrinated with the kind of self-esteemism that deliberately teaches them to believe they are never actually in the wrong, no matter what. Many celebrities in the entertainment world have the act down pat. Most of them nowadays are nowhere as sophisticated or outwardly decent as the Pharisees were, but they are equally convinced that if there is anything wrong in their lives, it must be someone else's fault. I even saw a convicted pedophile and serial killer interviewed from his prison cell on the news one night. Asked why he decided to grant an interview, he said, "I want people to know I am not a bad guy."

Sinful hearts have an amazing capacity for self-deception, and you see that dynamic at work in the rank audacity of this elder son. He was totally convinced that he *deserved* everything the father had given to the son who admitted he deserved nothing.

Ironically, even as he was making that protest, the elder son was demonstrating by his actions that he had no love for the father, no interest in the father's love for his younger brother, no desire to participate in his father's joy—and no joy of his own about anything. He said he felt like a slave in his own household. He had clearly treasured up a heart full of resentment against his father. His heart was wretched. He was clearly as alienated from the father as his Prodigal brother had ever been. How could someone so thoroughly miserable honestly insist that he was perfect and without any need for repentance? Such is the self-deception of sin.

> The elder son was demonstrating by his actions that he had no love for the father, no interest in the father's love for his younger brother, no desire to participate in his father's joy—and no joy of his own about anything.

But he wasn't finished even yet. Next, he compared himself to the father, and naturally, in his eyes, the father fell far short: "You never gave me a young goat, that I might make merry with my friends" (v. 29). In other words, "Your other son comes home after causing you public disgrace, and you give him prime veal along with a party with the entire village. I work like a slave for you for years, and you haven't even given me enough goat meat for a small reception with a few of my closest friends."

That was not true, by the way. Remember, his father had given the elder son full rights to everything he owned. This false accusation is a thousand times more wicked than the elder son's insistence that he had nothing to ask his father's forgiveness for. Now he was actually suggesting that the father needed to seek *his* forgiveness.

The way the elder son described what he thought his father ought to have done for him may contain a further clue about his estrangement. Notice that if the father had given him a goat, his desire would have been to use it to "make merry with my friends." The honor he imagined—and insisted he deserved—was the privilege of partying with his own friends.

The elder brother's idea of the ideal party would not include his brother, his father, or their friends and neighbors. He was living in a completely different world. He had a completely different group of friends. He might still have been sleeping at home, but his circle of relationships was a closed group that excluded his father, his brother, and the wider circle of the family's relationships. He sought fellowship and companionship instead from people who shared his values, and that definitely excluded the father. (Incidentally, even that characteristic of the elder brother mirrors the attitude of the Pharisees. They strictly excluded from their circle of fellowship all who did not see eye to eye with them.)

What we see here is an angry, resentful, envious, impenitent, and greedy young man. This was not merely a bad response to the unexpected shock of the day's events; this was the elder brother's true character coming out.

HIS HOSTILITY TOWARD HIS BROTHER

Next this embittered son turned his acrimony against the returned Prodigal: "But as soon as this son of yours came, who has devoured your livelihood with harlots, you killed the fatted calf for him"

(v. 30). That, of course, was a further assault on his father's character, integrity, and virtue. He was still insinuating that his father had been grossly unjust.

But what is most remarkable about that statement is its utter lack of any regard for his own brother. In fact, he refused to refer to him as "my brother." Instead, he called him "this son of yours"—and then he purposely brought up the sins of the Prodigal and reviewed them all in living color—even though he knew very well that the father had already declared those sins forgiven.

It appears he purposely hauled out the most offensive sins and put those on the table first. He was naming sins for which, technically under the Mosaic principles of justice, death was deemed a just punishment (cf. Deuteronomy 21:18–21). It was his subtle way of stressing that the Prodigal Son *should* be dead and that he would frankly be happier if he were. This was an amazingly coldhearted and wicked attack on a son he knew the father loved—before the elder son had even shown the courtesy of greeting his brother and giving him an opportunity to express his repentance personally.

This was an egregious, unbrotherly attack on his younger brother. Remember, the elder brother had been perfectly content to see his rebellious brother demand his split of the inheritance early and leave home in the first place. He might not have technically been complicit in the Prodigal's rebellion, but neither had he been any kind of good influence on him.

The firstborn son ought to have been a role model for his younger sibling. And, indeed, perhaps he had been. It may well be that the Prodigal Son had learned his disrespect from his elder brother—but lacking the restraint that comes with maturity, he didn't learn when to quit and thus overtly took his rebellion down a path that almost ended in his destruction.

There is not a hint of sorrow about any of those things in the elder son's lament. He was concerned only about himself, his desires, his status, and his own self-love. He seemed to be suggesting that he would have been much happier if his brother had indeed died in the far country.

HIS INSENSIBILITY TO THE TRUTH

Even though it appears the father knew all along that the elder son's heart was not right, such a sudden barrage of coldhearted rebellion must have caught him a little off guard. It was a stark departure from the normal passive-aggressive style the boy had perfected.

But even in the wake of that verbal onslaught, the father responded with tenderness and a soft answer. He said to him, "Son, you are always with me, and all that I have is yours. It was right that we should make merry and be glad, for your brother was dead and is alive again, and was lost and is found" (Luke 15:31–32).

Eight times in this passage, the Greek text uses the word *huios*, the formal word for "son." Here, however, the father says *teknon*, meaning "my child." The father's tone was clearly full of grief and agonizing pain, mixed with compassionate love and mercy. He was still using the most endearing terms and making an amazingly gentle plea.

Remember, this son had addressed his father with no title, no name, no affection, and no respect: "Look! I have slaved for you." He had attacked the virtue, the integrity, the justice, and the righteousness of the father. The elder son was full of demands and devoid of any understanding. The father, by contrast (though he had the authority to command), made no appeal other than a gentle, reasonable plea.

Sometimes it is easier to be patient with prodigals than it is with hypocrites. As a pastor, I think of that often. Formerly down-and-out sinners who have been wonderfully and thoroughly converted are a true joy. They tend to be enthusiastic, eager to learn, full of gratitude, and zealous about bringing others to Christ. The people who tend to cause their pastors the most grief almost always seem to be people who grew up in the church and learned early how to be hypocritical. The complainers, the critics, and the curmudgeons usually come from that group. It sometimes takes an extra measure of grace to respond rightly to these people. It is remarkable that the only Pharisee named in all the Gospels who became a follower of Christ was Nicodemus (John 19:39).

This father did that. He knew this son was estranged and unhappy, and instead of scolding him for his sour attitude, he simply reassured his first-born son of his love and affection, and reminded him of the riches that were already his. If he wanted a relationship with his father, it was his for the asking. If he had any needs, the resources were already there for the taking: "All that I have is yours" (v. 31). That was literally the case, and it had always been. This son had full usufructuary rights to everything on the property. His inheritance—which included everything the father had—was already available for him to use any way he liked.

> Sometimes it is easier to be patient with prodigals than it is with hypocrites.

There is no sign the elder son responded to the gentle pleas of his father. By all appearances, his heart remained as cold as stone.

So the father made one final plea, and it was a full reiteration of the main theme that dominates all of Luke 15: "It was right that we should make merry and be glad, for your brother was dead and is alive again, and was lost and is found" (v. 32).

As far as the father was concerned, the celebration was perfectly right and natural. His lost son had returned a different person. It was like receiving someone back from the dead. They *had* to celebrate that. There was no alternative: "We *had* to be merry and rejoice" (NASB). It would have been wrong *not* to celebrate.

The unspoken implication should have touched the elder son's heart: "We will celebrate for you, too, if you come."

The father's perspective was the exact reverse of the elder brother's. Did you notice that? Whereas the son acted as if he would have been happier for his brother to be dead, the father, who had long ago reckoned the Prodigal as good as dead and grieved over him for many days with a broken heart, was overjoyed to have him back alive. He could not understand his eldest son's attitude—because frankly, it made no sense.

THE SPIRITUAL STRUGGLE

This closing scene of Jesus' drama is quite surreal. The exchange between a loving father and his estranged son is deliberately juxtaposed against a celebration that represents heaven's supreme joy. The contrasts are stark and shocking. Inside, there is a vibrant celebration, with music, dancing, a feast, and a beloved son who is gloriously redeemed.

But out in the dark of the night, a spiritual struggle is taking place. While everyone else in the village was inside honoring the father, his own son had dragged him outside to heap contempt on him. The older brother, in the gall of his own bitterness, had just attacked the virtue, the integrity, and the character of his own loving father. It was as if every embittered thought he had ever locked away in his heart over all those years suddenly exploded out of him. His mask was torn off. His cover was blown.

Nevertheless, the father responded, as always, with grace, mercy, tenderness, compassion, and rich, pure love. The ball was now in the elder son's court. How would he respond?

That is where Jesus' telling of the parable ended—outside the celebration, with no satisfying resolution to the story. The father's plea to the elder brother simply hung in the air, and the parable ended with a tender appeal for his repentance.

That is because the whole parable was told in the first place to make that entreaty stand out. It was really Jesus' own appeal to the

Pharisees—and to all others who think they are truly worthy of God's grace and favor.

If you, dear reader, are someone who thinks your own goodness will be sufficient to gain you a good standing before God, it is a plea that goes out to you also.

PART 5

The Epilogue

ELEVEN

The Shocking Real-Life Ending

Then, from that day on, they plotted to put Him to death.

—John 11:53

"YOUR BROTHER WAS DEAD AND IS ALIVE AGAIN, AND was lost and is found" (Luke 15:32).

With those words, the parable of the prodigal son ended—but like a musical arrangement without a final, satisfying chord resolution. No more words, and Jesus simply walked away from the public venue where He was teaching. He moved into a more private context with His own disciples, where He began to tell them a whole new parable. The narrative reflects the shift in Luke 16:1. "He also said to His disciples: 'There was a certain rich man . . .'"

This is stunning. The ending is the thing in every story. We wait with anticipation for the finale. It's so vital that some readers can't resist turning to the end to see how the plot resolves before they read the actual story. But this story leaves us hanging. In fact, the Prodigal Son's story ends so abruptly that a textual critic with a low view of Scripture might very well suggest that what we have here is just a story fragment, unaccountably unfinished by the author. Or is it more likely that the ending was written down but somehow separated from the original manuscript and lost forever? There surely must be an end to this story somewhere, right?

But the abruptness of the ending doesn't leave us without the point; it *is* the point. This is the final blow in a long series of shocks that were built into Jesus' telling of the story. Of all the surprising plot twists and startling details, this is the culminating surprise: Jesus marvelously shaped the point and then simply walked away without resolving the tension between the father and his firstborn. But there is no missing fragment. He intentionally left the story unfinished and the dilemma unsettled. It is *supposed* to make us feel like we're waiting for a punch line or final sentence.

> The abruptness of the ending is entirely deliberate.

Surely the people in Jesus' original audience were left standing with their mouths hanging open as He walked away. They must have asked one another the same question that is on the tip of our tongues when we read it today: *What happened? How did the elder son respond? What is the end of the story?* The Pharisees, of all people would want to know, because the elder son clearly represented them.

It's easy to imagine that the guests in the story would be eager to hear how everything turned out. They were all still inside at the celebration, waiting for the father to come back inside. When he left the party so abruptly, people would conclude that something serious was going on. In a real-life situation such as this, it would begin to be whispered around among the guests that the elder brother was out there, very angry that people were celebrating something as reprehensible as the immediate, unconditional, wholesale forgiveness of a son who had behaved as badly as the prodigal. Everyone would want to study the father's expression when he came back inside to try to detect some clue about what happened. That's exactly *our* response, as listeners to Jesus' story.

But with all that pent-up expectation, Jesus simply walked away, leaving the tale hanging, unfinished, unresolved.

Incidentally, Kenneth E. Bailey, a Presbyterian commentator who was fluent in Arabic and a specialist in Middle-Eastern literature (he spent forty years living and teaching the New Testament in Egypt, Lebanon, Jerusalem and Cyprus) provides a fascinating analysis of the literary style of the Prodigal Son's story.[1] The structure of the parable explains why Jesus left it unfinished. Bailey demonstrates that the parable divides naturally into two nearly equal parts, and each part is systematically structured in a kind of mirrored pattern (ABCD-DCBA) called a *chiasm*. It's a kind of parallelism that seems practically poetic, but it is a typical device in Middle Eastern prose to facilitate storytelling.

The first half—where the focus is completely on the younger brother—has eight stanzas or strophes, and in this case the parallels describe the prodigal's progress from departure to return:

Then He said: "A certain man had two sons.

A. Death—*And the younger of them said to his father, 'Father, give me the portion of goods that falls to me.' So he divided to them his livelihood.*

B. All Is Lost—*And not many days after, the younger son gathered all together, journeyed to a far country, and there wasted his possessions with prodigal living. But when he had spent all, there arose a severe famine in that land, and he began to be in want.*

C. Rejection—*Then he went and joined himself to a citizen of that country, and he sent him into his fields to feed swine. And he would gladly have filled his stomach with the pods that the swine ate, and no one gave him anything.*

D. The Problem—*But when he came to himself, he said, 'How many of my father's hired servants have bread enough and to spare, and I perish with hunger!*

D. The Solution—*I will arise and go to my father, and will say to him, "Father, I have sinned against heaven and before you, and I am no longer worthy to be called your son. Make me like one of your hired servants." And he arose and came to his father.*

C. **Acceptance**—*But when he was still a great way off, his father saw him and had compassion, and ran and fell on his neck and kissed him.*

B. **All Is Restored**—*And the son said to him, 'Father, I have sinned against heaven and in your sight, and am no longer worthy to be called your son.' But the father said to his servants, 'Bring out the best robe and put it on him, and put a ring on his hand and sandals on his feet.*

A. **Resurrection**—*And bring the fatted calf here and kill it, and let us eat and be merry; for this my son was dead and is alive again; he was lost and is found.' And they began to be merry."*

The second half shifts focus to the elder brother and progresses through a similar chiastic pattern. But it ends abruptly after the seventh strophe:

A. **He Stands Aloof**—*"Now his older son was in the field. And as he came and drew near to the house, he heard music and dancing. So he called one of the servants and asked what these things meant.*

B. **Your Brother; Peace (a feast); Anger**— *And he said to him, 'Your brother has come, and because he has received him safe and sound, your father has killed the fatted calf.' But he was angry and would not go in.*

C. **Costly Love**—*Therefore his father came out and pleaded with him.*

D. **My Actions, My Pay**—*So he answered and said to his father, 'Lo, these many years I have been serving you; I never transgressed your commandment at any time; and yet you never gave me a young goat, that I might make merry with my friends.*

D. **His Actions, His Pay**—*'But as soon as this son of yours came, who has devoured your livelihood with harlots, you killed the fatted calf for him.'*

C. **Costly Love**—*And he said to him, 'Son, you are always with me, and all that I have is yours.*

B. Your Brother; Safe (a feast); Joy!— *It was right that we should make merry and be glad, for your brother was dead and is alive again, and was lost and is found.'"*

A. The Missing Ending

The end of the parable is deliberately asymmetrical, as if to put extra stress on the lack of resolution. The ending simply isn't there.

We're *supposed* to notice that. Since the story stops abruptly with such a tender appeal, every hearer ought to take that plea to heart, meditate on it, personalize it, and see the gentle reasonableness of embracing the father's joy in the salvation of sinners. And, frankly, no one needed that sort of honest self-examination more than the legalistic scribes and Pharisees to whom Jesus told the story. The parable was an invitation first of all for them to forsake their pride and self-righteousness and reconcile with God's way of salvation. But furthermore, the same principle applies to everyone else, too—from wanton sinners like the Prodigal Son to sanctimonious hypocrites like the elder brother, and all kinds of people in between. Thus everyone who hears the story writes his or her own ending by how we respond to the kindness of God toward sinners.

> Everyone who hears the story writes his or her own ending by how we respond to the kindness of God toward sinners.

It is an ingenious way to end the story. It leaves us wanting to pen the ending we would like to see. Anyone whose heart is not already hardened by self-righteous resentment ought to apprehend in the parable something about the glory of God's grace in Christ—especially His loving forgiveness and glad-hearted acceptance of penitent sinners. The person who catches even a glimpse of that truth would surely want to write something good—like this:

Then the elder son fell on his knees before his father, saying, "I repent for my bitter, loveless heart, for my hypocritical service, and for my pride and self-righteousness. Forgive me, Father. Make me a true son, and take me inside to the feast." The father then embraced his first-born son, smothered him with tearful, grateful kisses, took him inside, and seated him alongside his brother in dual seats of honor. They all rejoiced together and the level of joy that already amazing celebration suddenly doubled. No one there would ever forget that night.

That would be the perfect ending. But I can't write the ending for anyone else—including the scribes and Pharisees. They wrote their own ending, and it was nothing at all like that one.

THE TRAGIC ENDING

Don't forget that Jesus told this parable—including the abrupt ending—chiefly for the benefit of the scribes and Pharisees. It was really a story about them. The elder brother represented them. The hanging resolution underscored the truth that the next move was theirs. The father's final tender plea was Jesus' own gentle appeal to them.

> The Pharisees' ultimate response to Jesus would write the end of the story in real-life.

If they had demanded to know the end of the parable on the spot, Jesus might well have said to them, "That is up to you." The Pharisees' ultimate response to Jesus would write the end of the story in real-life.

We therefore know how the tale really ended, then, don't we? It is not a happy ending. Instead, it's another shocking plot turn. In fact, it is the greatest shock and outrage of all time.

They killed Him.

Since the father figure in the parable represents Christ and the elder brother is a symbol of Israel's religious elite, in effect, the true ending to the story, as written by the scribes and Pharisees them-selves, ought to read something like this: "The elder son was out-raged at his father. He picked up a piece of lumber and beat him to death in front of everyone."

I told you it was a shocking ending.

You may be thinking to yourself, *No! That's not how the story ends. I grew up hearing that parable in Sunday school, and it's not sup-posed to have a tragic ending.*

Indeed, it seems like any rational person whose mind and heart is not utterly twisted by his own sanctimonious hypocrisy would listen to such a parable with deep joy and holy thankfulness for the generous grace that lifts a fallen sinner up, restores him to whole-ness, and receives him again into his father's favor. Any humble-hearted individual who sees himself reflected in the Prodigal would naturally enter into the father's joy and celebration, rejoic-ing that Jesus would paint such a vivid portrait of divine grace. As we've seen from the very start, the clear message of the parable is about how eagerly Jesus receives sinners. It should end with joy, not tragedy. Everyone should join the celebration.

But the elder brother's heart was clearly (albeit secretly until now) hardened against his father. He had stored up years worth of resent-ment, anger, greed, and self-will—while wearing his father's favor as a badge of legitimacy. He never really understood or appreciated his father's goodness to him; but he was happy to receive it and milk it for whatever he could get out of it. He completely misinterpreted his father's kindness, thinking it was proof of his own worthiness; when in reality it was an expression of *the father's* goodness. And as soon as the father showed such lavish favor to the utterly unworthy prodigal brother, the elder brother's resentment quickly boiled over and his true character could not be concealed any longer.

Remember, the elder brother is a picture of the Pharisees. His attitude mirrored theirs exactly. If the elder son's behavior seems appalling and hard to understand for you and me, it was not at all hard to understand for the Pharisees. They were steeped in a religious system that cultivated precisely that kind of self-righteous, self-congratulatory, self-willed perspective with respect to the goodness and grace of God. They believed they had God's favor because they had earned it, pure and simple. So when Jesus showed favor to repentant tax collectors, prostitutes, and other lowlifes who clearly did not deserve any favor, the Pharisees resented it. They believed Jesus' kindness toward lowly sinners took the sheen off the emblem of their superiority, and they became angry in precisely the same way the elder son became angry.

Does it not seem remarkable that when Jesus brought his telling of the parable to such an abrupt halt—leaving off the ending completely—Luke's account is utterly silent regarding any kind of response from the Pharisees? They knew full well that the message of the parable was aimed at them and ought to have shamed them. But they asked no questions, made no protest, offered no commentary, asked for no further elaboration. The reason is that they understood the elder brother's attitude already. It made perfect sense to them. Perhaps they didn't even feel the lack of resolution to the same degree most listeners do, because to them the elder brother's complaint seemed perfectly reasonable. The way they would have *liked* to see the story resolved required *the father's* repentance. In their ideal scenario, the father would see the elder son's point, make a public apology to the elder son, publicly shame the Prodigal for his foolish behavior, and then perhaps even cast the Prodigal out forever. But the Pharisees surely saw the point Jesus was making clearly enough that they knew the story would never take a turn like *that*.

So they said nothing—at least nothing Luke (guided by the Holy Spirit) deemed important enough to record for us. Perhaps they simply turned and walked away. More likely, Jesus turned away from them.

In fact, let's assume there's no ellipsis at this point in the chronology of Luke's narrative. Luke 15 ends where the parable of the Prodigal Son ends. But Luke 16 continues with Jesus still speaking. This seems to be the record of one lengthy discourse. And in Luke 16:1, Jesus does indeed turn away from the scribes and Pharisees "to the disciples," and He begins to instruct them with another parable. This one is about the shrewdness of unbelievers and the impossibility of serving both God *and* money. Luke 16:14 says, "Now the Pharisees, who were lovers of money, also heard all these things, and they derided Him"—meaning they ridiculed Him.

So apparently they hung around, perhaps just on the periphery, after the parable of the Prodigal Son abruptly ended, undeterred in their opposition to Jesus. In fact, they were more determined than ever to silence Him, no matter what it took. And that attitude is what led them to write for themselves the tragic ending to the greatest parable of all time.

The Pharisees' hatred for Jesus grew from the day he told them the parable until they hatched a conspiracy to kill Him. "And the chief priests and the scribes sought how they might take Him by trickery and put Him to death" (Mark 14:1). In the end, they secured the grudging cooperation of the Roman authorities, and even the collusion of Herod—and they had Him crucified.

Christ's death on the cross occurred at their urging just a few months after this encounter in Luke 15. Then they congratulated themselves on a righteous act that they were certain would preserve the honor of Israel and the true religion they believed was embodied in their beloved traditions.

THE GLORIOUS SEQUEL

Here is the divine irony: when they did their worst, they accomplished God's best (Acts 2:22; 2 Corinthians 5:21; Isaiah 53). But even Jesus' death was not the end of the story. No grave could hold Jesus in its grip. He rose from the dead, signifying that He had conquered sin, guilt, and death once and for all. His dying on the cross finally produced the effectual blood atonement that had been shrouded in mystery for all the ages, and His resurrection was the proof that God accepted it.

> The invitation to be part of the great celebratory banquet is still open to all. It extends even to you, dear reader.

Jesus' death therefore provided for us what the blood of bulls and goats could never accomplish: a full and acceptable atonement for sin. And His perfect righteousness gives us precisely what we need for our redemption: a complete covering of perfect righteousness equal to God's own divine perfection.

So there *is* true and blessed resolution to the story after all.

THE OPEN INVITATION

The invitation to be part of the great celebratory banquet is still open to all. It extends even to you, dear reader. And it doesn't matter whether you are an open sinner like the Prodigal Son, a secret one like his elder brother, or someone with characteristics from each type. If you are someone who is still estranged from God, Christ urges you to acknowledge your guilt, admit your own spiritual poverty, embrace your heavenly Father, and be reconciled to Him (2 Corinthians 5:20).

> And the Spirit and the bride say, "Come!" And let him who hears say, "Come!" And let him who thirsts come. Whoever desires, let him take the water of life freely. (Revelation 22:17)

Now, enjoy the celebration.

⟨ APPENDIX ⟩

Storied Truth: Learning to Find Meaning in Parables

It has been given to you to know the mysteries . . .

—Matthew 13:11

WHAT IS THE SIGNIFICANCE OF JESUS' USE OF STORIES as a medium for His teaching? Thirty years ago, the typical evangelical could have easily answered that question in three sentences or less. As a matter of fact, it is not really a difficult question at all, because Jesus Himself answered it plainly when said He employed parables for a dual reason: to illustrate the truth for those who were willing to receive it and to obscure the truth from those who hated it anyway:

> But when He was alone, those around Him with the twelve asked Him about the parable. And He said to them, "To you it has been given to know the mystery of the kingdom of God; but to those who are outside, all things come in parables, so that 'Seeing they may see and not perceive, And hearing they may hear and not understand; Lest they should turn, And their sins be forgiven them.'" (Mark 4:10–12)

So the short, simple answer to our opening question is that Jesus' parables are tools with which He taught and defended the *truth*.

Do a simple survey and you'll notice that when Jesus explained His own parables to the disciples, He always did so by giving definite, objective meanings for the symbols He used: "The seed is the word of God" (Luke 8:11). "The field is the world" (Matthew 13:38). Sometimes His symbolism is perfectly obvious without any explanation, such as the shepherd in Luke 15:4–7 (who is obviously a figure of Christ Himself). Other times the meaning takes a little more careful thought and exegesis, but the true meaning can still be understood and explained clearly. A little bit of hard work and careful thinking always yields rich rewards in the study of parables. That, of course, is the very thing I have endeavored to do throughout this book.

Whether the true meaning of this or that symbol is patently obvious or one that requires a little detective work, the point is still the same: Jesus' parables were all *illustrative* of gospel facts. The stories were not (as some people nowadays like to suggest) creative alternatives to propositional truth statements, designed to supplant certainty. They were not dreamy fantasies told merely to evoke a feeling. And they certainly weren't mind games contrived to make everything vague. Much less was Jesus employing fictional forms in order to displace truth itself with mythology.

Above all, He was not inviting His hearers to interpret the stories any way they liked and thus let each one's own personal opinions be the final arbiter of what is true for that person. The conviction that the Bible itself is the final rule of faith (and the corresponding belief that Scripture itself should govern how we interpret Scripture) is a longstanding canon of biblical Christianity. Deny it, and you have in effect denied the authority of Scripture.

That's not to suggest that all Scripture is *equally* clear. Some of the parables in particular are notoriously difficult to interpret. It takes care, hard work, and the Holy Spirit's help to get it right. No one has ever seriously disputed that.

But on the question of whether each parable actually *has* a single divinely inspired sense and therefore a proper interpretation—an *objectively* true sense—there has never been any serious dispute among people who take the authority of Scripture seriously. The corollary of that idea is an equally sound principle: every possible interpretation that contradicts the one true meaning of a passage is false by definition.

In these postmodern times, however, there seems to be an abundance of voices denying those simple principles. They often suggest that since Jesus made such lavish use of parables and storytelling in His public ministry, He must not have thought of truth the same way modern men and women think of it. Is truth ultimately an objective reality—fixed and immutable, or is it soft and pliable and subjective?

This is more than just an interesting footnote to the rest of the book. It's a crucial matter to raise and examine—especially just now. We live in a generation where traces of fact and reality are sometimes deliberately blended together with elements of myth, guesswork, theory, falsehood, fiction, and feeling—and then released in the form of a dark mist in order to make the concept of *truth* itself seem like a murky, mysterious vapor with no real substance.

Some who actually prefer this cloudy notion of truth are trying to tell us Jesus took precisely that approach to teaching. They say the main reason He frequently turned to storytelling was to stress the inscrutability of divine truth and thereby confound the spiritual arrogance and hypocrisy of His day. The Pharisees, for example, thought they had truth all figured out—even though they did not agree with the equally overconfident Sadducees. Jesus' parables simply put the whole concept of truth right back where it belongs: in the unfathomable realm of sheer mystery.

At least that's what those who have drunk deeply from the postmodern spirit of our age would have us believe. They insist it is a mistake to subject our Lord's narratives to serious systematic analysis in search of a precise interpretation because to do that is to miss the real purpose of the stories. Instead, we're told, it's better to enjoy and admire and adapt Jesus' stories in whatever way makes them most meaningful to us. According to this way of thinking, since stories are inherently subjective, we should be less concerned with asking what the parables *mean*—and more concerned with finding ways of making the stories of the Bible our own.[1]

I was recently shown an essay posted on the Internet by an anonymous author (presumably a pastor) who reimagined the parable of the prodigal son from a feminist perspective and thereby intentionally turned the entire story on its head. In this person's freehanded reinterpretation, we're encouraged to visualize the father as an aloof family patriarch who thoughtlessly drives his younger son away by neglect. This one new facet of the story "changes everything," the unknown writer solemnly informs us. The son's demand for the early inheritance now "alludes to a prior and perhaps long-standing family strain, [and] the boy's dissolute living may be his effort to 'buy' . . . affiliation and belonging," which he had long craved but did not have because the father had so carelessly marginalized him. Rather than a self-indulgent "plot to sow his wild oats," the Prodigal's pursuit of a reckless lifestyle thus becomes a desperate cry for help.[2]

Further observing that Jesus' own telling of the prodigal son parable ends without resolution, the article suggests that this "reveals the open-endedness of the Kingdom of God." What's more, the story's *true* ending "is the end of my story, your story, and everyone's story—beyond our wildest dreams."[3]

By such a wholly subjective approach, Jesus' stories become playthings to be bent and shaped into whatever form suits the hearer's fancy. Jesus' whole message becomes versatile, subjective, and infinitely adaptable to the felt needs and personal preferences of each hearer.

That is a very popular way to deal with Jesus' teaching these days: as if His parables were given mainly to create a mood and set the stage for a billion uniquely personal dramas. It's okay to admire the setting, but it's not okay to hold the story up to the light and attempt to discover any objective or universal meaning in it. Instead, we are supposed to try to experience the story for ourselves by living within it, or by retelling it in our own words, using little more than our imaginations. That's how we can make Jesus' stories into *our* stories. It means, in effect, that the interpretation, the lesson, and the ending of each story are ultimately ours to determine.

In contemporary academic circles, such an approach would be recognized as a rather extreme form of *narrative theology*. That's a fashionable buzzword these days, used to describe a large family of novel ideas about how we should interpret the Bible (with special emphasis on the "story" rather than the truth claims of Scripture). The stylishness of narrative theology has led to vast amounts of discussion—and a considerable measure of confusion—about Jesus' role as a storyteller. What did He mean to convey in His stories? Why did He use so many parables? How are we supposed to understand them? Does the narrative form itself alter or nullify the normal rules for interpreting Scripture?

On an even broader scale, does Jesus' frequent use of stories constitute a valid argument against the systematic approach to doctrine Christians have historically taken? Do we really even *need* to analyze Scripture, categorize truth, and attempt to understand biblical doctrine in any kind of logical fashion—or is it okay just to appreciate the stories and embellish them with our own plot twists and real-life endings? In very simple terms: is Jesus' own style of teaching actually incompatible with our doctrinal statements, confessions of faith, and systematic approach to theology?

Those are all important questions, but they are not difficult to answer if we simply accept at face value what the Bible itself says about Jesus' use of parables.

STORIES AS EFFECTIVE VEHICLES FOR TRUTH

Jesus was a master storyteller, but He never told a story merely for the story's sake. His parables weren't word games or do-it-yourself mysteries where each hearer was invited to provide his or her own meaning. Each of His parables had an important lesson to convey, originating with Christ Himself and built into the fabric of the parable by Him.

That is a crucial fact to keep in mind, because it explains how *truth* (as we understand the concept) is compatible with storytelling. Even pure fiction is not altogether incompatible with our conventional ideas of truth—because every well-told story ultimately makes a point. And the point of a good story is supposed to be true (or at least true to life on *some* level), even when the story itself paints a totally imaginary scenario.

That is the very nature of parables. It is the main reason that (as we discussed in the introduction to this book) one central lesson is always the most important feature of every parable and we should focus on that, rather than seeking hidden meaning in all the peripheral details of the story. When you see the key point of a parable, you have the essence of whatever truth the story aims to convey. That lesson itself is sometimes filled out or embellished by plot elements, characters, and other details in the story. But there's no need to look for multiple layers of meaning or suppose that some deeper symbolism or different dimension of truth has been hidden in the incidental features of the tale. As we noted in the introduction, parables aren't allegories, full of symbols from top to bottom. They highlight one important truth—just like the moral of a well-told story.

That explains why the vital truth contained in a parable is fixed and objective—not a metaphysical glob of modeling clay we can bend and shape however we like. Remember that when Jesus began to use parables in His public ministry, He got alone with the disciples and carefully explained the parable of the sower to them

(Matthew 13:18–23). It had a clear, simple, single, straightforward, *objective* meaning, and as Jesus explained it to them, He indicated that all the parables could be understood through a similar method of interpretation: "Do you not understand this parable? How then will you understand all the parables?" (Mark 4:13). Thus there is absolutely no reason to surmise that Jesus' use of parables is somehow an indication that truth itself is so entangled in mystery as to be utterly unknowable.

Quite the contrary: as we noted at the start of this appendix, Jesus used parables to make certain truths clear to believers while obscuring the meaning from unbelievers.

Have you ever considered *why* He did that? Obscuring the truth from unbelievers was (in a very important sense) an act of mercy, because the more truth they heard and spurned, the worse it would be for them in the final judgment.

But Jesus' use of parables was also itself a temporal sign of judgment against them, sealing their own stubborn unbelief by removing the light of truth from them. They had already hardened their own hearts: "For the hearts of this people have grown dull. Their ears are hard of hearing, and their eyes they have closed, lest they should see with their eyes and hear with their ears, lest they should understand with their hearts and turn, so that I should heal them" (Matthew 3:15). Unbelief can be irreversible. Jesus' use of parables both highlighted that reality and stood as a warning sign to all, encouraging us not to harden our hearts the way the Pharisees did, but rather to seek the truth.

Yet Jesus told the disciples, "Blessed are your eyes for they see, and your ears for they hear" (v. 16). Jesus was making it clear that the parables *do* have objective meaning, and that meaning can indeed be apprehended. "It has been given to you to know the mysteries of the kingdom" (Mark 4:11). Thus He plainly indicated that the parables contained eternal, spiritual truth that can actually be seen and heard and *known* by anyone with spiritual eyes and ears.

So even though the parables concealed Jesus' meaning from *unbelievers*, it's not as if He was forever encasing the truth itself in hopeless, impenetrable mystery. Truth is actually being unveiled and illustrated in every one of His parables. It is vital, timeless, unchanging, unadulterated, and unequivocal truth—not some ethereal or inaccessible truth. On the contrary, it is all simple enough that any believer through the due use of ordinary means should be able to come to a sound and sure understanding of it.

THE WEALTH OF TRUTH IN JESUS' PARABLES

Jesus' stories were remarkable for both their simplicity and their sheer abundance. In Matthew and Luke, multiple parables are sometimes given in rapid-fire fashion, one after another, with little or no interpretive or elaborative material interspersed between them. Extended discourses containing virtually nothing but parables sometimes fill chapter-length portions of Matthew and Luke. (See, for example, Matthew 13; Matthew 24:32–25:30; and of course, Luke 15:4–16:13.) The selections recorded by Matthew and Luke were probably representative samples rather than exhaustive catalogues of Jesus' parables. Nevertheless, it seems reasonable to conclude that the parable-upon-parable pattern closely approximates Jesus' actual style of discourse.

Jesus clearly *liked* to teach by telling stories rather than by giving a list of raw facts for rote memorization or by outlining information in a neatly catalogued systematic layout. He was never stiff and pedantic when He taught, but always informal and conversational. The parables contained familiar figures, and sometimes they stirred raw emotions. These things were what made Jesus' preaching most memorable, rather than tidy lists or clever alliteration.

That's not a novel observation, by the way; it's a fact that stands out on the face of the New Testament text—especially in the three synoptic Gospels (Matthew, Mark, and Luke). And of course, all four Gospels plus the book of Acts are likewise recorded almost completely in narrative form. In certain academic circles today, the sudden burst of enthusiasm over "narrative theology" and "narrative preaching" might give some students the impression that scholars have only recently discovered the Bible is full of stories. Read some recent books and journals on the subject, and you might even come away with the idea that the church has been kept largely in the dark (at least since the dawn of the modern era) until scholars reading the Bible through postmodern lenses suddenly noticed the true implications of Christ's narrative style of teaching.

Actually, Jesus' preference for narrative devices has been duly noted and strongly emphasized by practically every competent teacher in the history of the church, starting with the Gospel writers themselves, through the best of the early church fathers, down to and including practically every important Protestant biblical commentator of the past four centuries.

But the fact that Jesus showed such a preference for narrative forms *still* doesn't nullify either the didactic purpose of the parables or the unchanging truth they were meant to convey.

In fact, Matthew 13:34–35 sums up the proper perspective on the parables and their truth-value in very simple terms: "Jesus spoke to the multitude in parables; and without a parable He did not speak to them, that it might be fulfilled which was spoken by the prophet, saying: 'I will open My mouth in parables; I will utter things kept secret from the foundation of the world.'" He was quoting Psalm 78:2–4, which describe the primary purpose of the parables as a means of *revelation*, not *obfuscation*. The only context in which the parables deliberately conceal the truth or cloak it in mystery is in the face of willful, hostile unbelief.

STORIES AND PROPOSITIONS

One vital and related issue needs to be addressed briefly in this discussion, and that's the question of whether we violate the whole point of Jesus' storytelling when we summarize the truths we learn from the parables and restate them in propositional form.

That's a question frequently raised by people who take their cues from popular postmodernity. They conceive of *stories* and *propositions* as completely separate categories—virtually contradictory ways of thinking about truth. In the words of one author, "The emerging gospel of the electronic age is moving beyond cognitive *propositions* and linear formulas to embrace the power and truth of *story*."[4]

According to that way of thinking, the truth-value of a story cannot and should not be reduced to a mere proposition.

Propositions are the building blocks of logic. They are inherently simple, not complex. A proposition is nothing more than an assertion that either affirms or denies something. "Jesus Christ is Lord of all" (cf. Acts 10:36) is a classic biblical proposition that expresses one of the foundational truths of all Christian doctrine. Another is "There is no salvation in any other" (cf. Acts 4:12). The first example is an affirmation of Jesus' supremacy and exclusivity; the second is a denial of the converse. Both are simple propositions declaring the same basic biblical truth, but in slightly different ways.

The truth-value of every proposition is binary: it can only be either true or false. There is no middle value. And there is the rub as far as postmodern thinking is concerned: propositions do not allow for any ambiguity.

Since the form of a proposition demands either an affirmation or denial, and postmodern thinking prefers obscurity and vagueness rather than clarity, it is no wonder that the very notion of propositional truth has fallen out of favor in these postmodern times. Stories, by contrast, are widely perceived as fluid, subjective, and not necessarily emphatic—just like the postmodernist view of truth itself.

So it is more and more common these days to hear people express the belief that the brand of truth embodied in stories is somehow of an altogether different nature from the kind of truth that we can express in propositions. What they generally are arguing for is a fluid, subjective, ambiguous concept of truth itself.

To embrace that perspective is in effect to make mincemeat of the very notion of truth. Truth cannot be verbally expressed or formally affirmed at all—even in story form—without recourse to propositions. So the postmodern attempt to divorce truth from propositions is nothing more than a way of talking about truth, toying with the idea of truth, and giving lip service to the existence of truth—without actually needing to affirm anything as true or deny anything as false.

That is why the church has historic creeds and confessions in the first place—and they are all chock-full of propositions. I've heard Al Mohler say repeatedly that while the biblical notion of truth is always *more* than propositional, it is never *less*. He is right. We are not to think Jesus' use of stories and parables in any way diminishes the importance of accuracy, clarity, historical facts, objective realities, sound doctrine, or propositional truth claims.

As a matter of fact, not all of Jesus' parables were full-fledged stories. Some of the shortest ones were stated in straightforward, simple propositional form. "The kingdom of heaven is like leaven, which a woman took and hid in three measures of meal till it was all leavened" (Matthew 13:33). Or, "Every scribe instructed concerning the kingdom of heaven is like a householder who brings out of his treasure things new and old" (v. 52). And, "[The kingdom] is like a mustard seed, which a man took and put in his garden; and it grew and became a large tree, and the birds of the air nested in its branches" (Luke 13:19).

Furthermore, propositions are used as building blocks in every one of the parables Jesus gave in extended story form. Take the parable of the prodigal son, for example. The very first sentence, "A certain man had two sons," is a simple proposition. The closing phrase of the parable is likewise a bare-bones proposition: "Your brother was dead and is alive again, and was lost and is found" (v. 32). Those are statements about the facts of the story rather than the central truth claim the story aims to teach, but they serve to illustrate that it is hardly possible to communicate either raw truth or complex story at all without using propositions. Moreover, it's well-nigh impossible to think of a truth that's authentically *knowable* that isn't capable of being expressed in propositional form.

To give another example, consider once more the three harmonious parables of Luke 15 (the lost sheep, the lost coin, and the prodigal son). The only exposition Jesus offers as a clue to their meaning is a single propositional statement: "There will be more joy in heaven over one sinner who repents than over ninety-nine just persons who need no repentance" (Luke 15:7). That, as we stressed throughout the body of this book, is the central theme and the key verse of this extended section of Scripture.

Notice: *that verse states a truth that is by definition objective*. It describes what occurs in heaven when someone repents. It discloses a reality that is not in any way affected by any person's individual perspective. On the contrary, it is a fact that is true regardless of how someone perceives it. In fact, it has been true from the beginning, before any earthly creature perceived it at all. That is precisely what we mean when we say truth is "objective."

Why is all this important? Because truth itself is critically important, and the church today is in imminent danger of selling her birthright in exchange for a postmodern philosophy that in effect would do away with the very idea of truth.

That is ground we cannot yield. We must be willing to submit our minds to the truth of Scripture, and we must refuse to subject Scripture to whatever theories or speculations happen to be currently popular in the realm of secular philosophy.

Beware lest anyone cheat you through philosophy and empty deceit, according to the tradition of men, according to the basic principles of the world, and not according to Christ.

—Colossians 2:8

❧ NOTES ❧

Chapter 4: His Shameful Misconduct

1. William Manchester, *A World Lit Only by Fire* (New York: Little, Brown, 1992), 54.

Chapter 6: His Return

1. D. Martyn Lloyd-Jones, *Out of the Depths* (Wheaton: Crossway, 1995), 57–58.

Chapter 7: His Forgiveness

1. Kenneth E. Bailey, *Finding the Lost Cultural Keys to Luke 15* (St. Louis: Concordia, 1992), 146.

Chapter 11: The Shocking Real-Life Ending

1. Kenneth E. Bailey, *Finding the Lost: Cultural Keys to Luke 15* (St. Louis: Concordia, 1992), 110, 164.

Appendix: Storied Truth: Learning to Find Meaning in Parables

1. I've responded in much greater detail to the current wave of postmodern influences among evangelicals in *The Truth War* (Nashville: Nelson, 2007).

2. The essay, titled "Check Out This Chick-Flick," was posted anonymously at the blog of First Trinity Lutheran Church (ELCA), Indianapolis; http://firsttrinitylutheran.blogspot.com/2007/03/check-out-this-chick-flick.html/.

3. Ibid.

4. Shane Hipps, *The Hidden Power of Electronic Culture* (Grand Rapids: Zondervan/Youth Specialties, 2006), 90; emphasis added.

❦ ABOUT THE AUTHOR ❧

John MacArthur is the pastor-teacher of Grace Community Church in Sun Valley, California, president of the Master's University and Seminary, and featured teacher with the Grace to You media ministry. Grace to You radio, video, audio, print, and website resources reach millions worldwide each day. In more than four decades of ministry, John has written dozens of bestselling books, including the MacArthur New Testament Commentary series, *The Gospel According to Jesus, Twelve Ordinary Men, Twelve Extraordinary Women, Slave,* and *The MacArthur Study Bible.* He and his wife, Patricia, have four married children and fifteen grandchildren.

For more details about John MacArthur and his Bible-teaching resources, contact Grace to You at 800-55-GRACE or www.gty.org.

John MacArthur
Unleashing God's Truth, One Verse at a Time®
A Trademark of Grace to You

❧ TOPICAL INDEX ❧

❧ SCRIPTURE INDEX ❧

219

9 781400 202683